THE SECOND TRUTH

THE

SECOND TRUTH

A Brief Introduction to the Intellectual and

Spiritual Journey that is Philosophy

James P. Danaher

PARAGON HOUSE

First Edition 2014

Published in the United States by
Paragon House
1925 Oakcrest Avenue, Suite 7
St. Paul, MN 55113

www.ParagonHouse.com

Library of Congress Cataloging-in-Publication Data

Danaher, James P.
The second truth : a brief, 21st century introduction to the intellectual and spiritual journey that is philosophy / James P. Danaher.
    pages cm
    Summary: "Contrasts the conceptual understanding we inherit from our culture and language community (first truth) with the more sophisticated understanding we gain through personal experience, searching, and philosophical questioning (second truth). Socrates and Jesus are described as persons who are exemplary in application of their second truths"--Provided by publisher.
    ISBN 978-1-55778-912-9 (paperback)
    1. Philosophy. 2. Religion. I. Title.
    BD21.D35 2014
    100--dc23
                        2013045157

Manufactured in the United States of America

10 9 8 7 6 5 4 3 2 1

The paper used in this publication meets the minimum requirements of American National Standard for Information Sciences—Permanence of Paper for Printed Library Materials, ANSIZ39.48-1984.

Dedicated to Pastor Floyd Nicholson who gave me my foundations but always encouraged me to seek a deep understanding.

Acknowledgment

I would like to acknowledge my indebtedness to Willard Pottinger whose proofreading, editing, insightful comments, and encouragement have greatly enhanced this work.

Contents

PREFACE

"What is Truth?"[1]

WE TAKE TRUTH to refer to ultimate reality, but although we acknowledge that there is such a reality, our experience of it is always filtered through an understanding that is unique to our species. No creatures perceive things as they are in themselves but rather as those creatures are equipped to perceive them. Ducks perceive the world differently than do ants, and whales differently than human beings. Human beings, however, are unique in the animal kingdom in that in addition to whatever natural hardware we have been given, we also process and filter the data of our experience through a conceptual understanding that is provided by a language that is passed onto us by our particular history and culture.

God or nature may have given us the ability to use language but the language that we use to interpret our world is largely the product of human judgments and conventions passed onto us by our history, culture, and language community. Over the last two hundred years, we have become ever more aware of the fact that language does not mirror nature, and this should come as no surprise since the ancients told us of this as well. In

---

1. John 18:38.

the major religions of the West there is the story of a fall from our natural, or original, God-given state. That fall includes the fall of language, to which the story of Babel specifically refers.[2] In a global society, we are more than ever before aware of how people from different historical epochs, and different cultures and language communities conceptualize the world differently. Perhaps some may still imagine that the understanding through which they interpret their experience is God-given, and therefore they interpret their experience as God intends them to interpret it, but that is a very difficult position to reasonably maintain and defend today. We now know that most of the concepts that we inherit as our initial understanding and through which we organize and make sense of our experience had their origin in the human judgments and conventions of past generations. Once those concepts are accepted into our culture and become part of our history, they are passed onto us through language acquisition. Consequently, when we speak of truth today we must consider the truth of the understanding through which we interpret the data of our experience. When we consider that truth, what we discover is not a single truth but rather two truths at the core of our human experience, both of which are absolutely true.

The first truth is our initial orientation to the world that we receive at our mother's knee and by which we learn how to divide the world into the kinds of things that our human community has agreed upon. Without this essential truth we have no orientation to the human world and no means of making sense

---

2. Genesis 11:1-9.

of it. It is essential to our psychological development and social wellbeing that we embrace this initial understanding as truth, since it provides a needed foundation for our psychological and social development. This initial understanding is also received as true simply by the fact that young children have little or no basis from which to critically assess what is being presented to them.

As we mature, however, there comes a time in most of our lives when we begin to question the truth of that initial understanding and set out in search of a second truth. We often get our first glimpse of the second truth when some event or circumstance makes it difficult to believe any longer in our initial orientation to the world. It could begin with some liminal experience that shatters and does violence to our initial understanding, or simply that we can no longer ignore the anomalies in that initial understanding. It could even come about simply because we recognize the mythic and conventional nature of that first truth, and that a myriad of alternative understandings exist. Whatever the circumstance, at such a point, we begin to explore the possibility of a second truth that might afford us a more meaningful interpretation of our experience than the view we inherited.

This book is about that second truth and the intellectual and spiritual journey that is our pursuit of it. The nature of this second truth is philosophical and very different from the nature of the truth of our initial understanding. While the first truth offers us firm foundations that we can hold on to, the second, philosophical truth is always out of reach. It is that more divine understanding that Socrates is always pursuing and, although he never attains it, it is what continually tells him that there is something wrong with his inherited orientation to the world and there is a better way to perceive and interpret things. This is the nature of the truth that drives people like Copernicus and Einstein to reject their inherited orientation and pursue an ever better perspective through which to interpret their experience. It is the truth that Jesus tells us to follow and what put him at odds with the religious leaders of his day.

Philosophical truth always puts us at odds with the truth of our cultural understanding, and with those people who defend inherited truth as the only truth. People with a need for security want a truth they can hold on to and feel secure in knowing, and the idea of a second truth threatens that security. Thus, there is a tension between those who cling to their inherited understanding and those on intellectual or spiritual journeys in pursuit of a second truth or better way to interpret their experience. The defenders of the first truth want to eliminate those in pursuit of a second truth, but our civilization has gone forward because of this mysterious second truth that tells us there is a still better way to think about what we are experiencing. It is that ever more divine perspective, the pursuit of which Socrates says makes us, "better, braver, and more active"[3] human beings. It is that mysterious truth that we never possess but that possesses us and tells us that there is always a better way to think about something.

These two truths create the tension that lies at the base of human history. This tension often results in violence as those who believe there is only one truth set out to destroy those in

---

3.   Plato. *Meno.* 86b5-c2.

pursuit of a second truth. People who cherish security above all else dismiss the call of the second truth and try to eliminate those in pursuit of it in order to maintain the certainty of their inherited, sacred understanding.

Of course, from a transcended perspective there is only one truth, but to suppose that our perspective replicates that truth exactly is either blasphemous or naïve. What is clear from our twenty-first century knowledge of the human condition is that our understanding of truth and God's understanding of truth are two different matters. Clearly, we do not perceive reality from the perspective of eternity, but from within the confines of our history, experience, and language communities. From within that context there is not one truth, but rather two essential truths that make for our dynamic human nature.

For those on intellectual or spiritual journeys the first truth may no longer be seen as sacred, but it is a truth that we never get completely beyond since it remains the basis for our inter-action with others throughout our lives. For those individuals in pursuit of a second truth, what is sacred is a truth that is always beyond them. It is a divine truth that keeps them in humble awe and fills them with wonder rather than knowledge. It is a truth that we never possess but which continually speaks to those who, like Socrates, have ears to hear a small voice within that tells them there is something wrong with their present under-standing and there is a better way to conceptualize what they are experiencing.

Human beings have a dynamic history because at the core of our human condition there are two truths and not one. It is not always a progressive history and sometimes the defenders of the inherited understanding win, but it is always a temporary victory, and the next generation will have a Socrates or two who see the worldview they have inherited for what it is and set out upon a journey in pursuit of what they hope to be a better way to conceptualize and interpret their experience. Some of their innovative concepts are part of the rubble of history, but some become part of the foundational truth of future generations.

Although these two truths are interrelated, and both are essential aspects of our human condition, they function very differently, and entail very different forms of intelligence. The first truth gives us our foundations, while the second draws us toward the fullness of life. The first truth is ultimately mythic although necessary to our wellbeing, while the second is mystical and equally essential to pursuing our human potential. The first is a truth that we can possess, but the second is a truth that possesses us. The first truth provides the safe harbor for our early stable development, but something deep within the human condition calls those who will listen to set out upon a journey after a mystical truth that is always out in front beckoning us to follow. The first truth is accessed through a form of intelligence that can accurately and quickly acquire information; the second is accessed through a discriminating intelligence and imagination that can allow the data of our experience to change the understanding through which we interpret that experience.

Those in pursuit of the second truth may at times naively believe that they have come to possess the ultimate perspective, but they are always proved wrong by future generations. The desire for a second truth may stem from our desire to know the world as it really is, but the full experience of the second truth humbles us and assures us that whatever new understanding we come to must be held lightly. We are finite creatures who lack God's infinite perspective but that does not mean that the second truth that we pursue is unknowable, but rather that it is infinitely knowable and we are never at the end of knowing that truth.

CHAPTER ONE

The Two Truths

WHEN I WAS A CHILD, I was a terrible student. When I got two D's on my report card my father was so pleased that I had passed two class he bought me a bike. They didn't have special ed back then for kids like me. Instead, they had the reading groups. There were The Blue Birds, The Yellow Birds, and I was always in another group that everyone knew: The Crows. Our books still had pictures and that big print. I never understood the big print. There was nothing wrong with our eyes; we were just thought to be slow. There was Billy Pizzapi, who ate paste, that little girl who smiled for no apparent reason, and me. For me the school year always ended in August, after summer school. I just wasn't very good at acquiring and retaining information—I'm still not—but somehow I became a philosopher, or maybe that's the very reason I became a philosopher.

I grew up, as most of us did, under the impression that intelligence was almost exclusively a matter of being able to record information quickly and accurately. I was certainly not quick and was often mistaken about what I was supposed to be learning. Years later, however, my discovery was that there is a form of intelligence that begins with the rejection of the way we were taught to interpret things. So maybe I wasn't as dumb as I looked; maybe I just had an intuition that there was some greater understanding or better way to interpret things. Whatever was the case, at a certain age the realization occurred to me that there was another truth in addition to what I had been given as my initial orientation to the world. This second truth was a truth that I did not possess, and perhaps never would, but it was a truth that I nevertheless had to pursue. The first step in that pursuit was to skeptically question what had been presented to me as true in my initial orientation to the world. What I had come to realize was that my initial orientation was not about the world itself but about how I should conceive of the world in order to have the same understanding as those of my culture, history, and language community. Such an orientation easily gives the illusion of being an objective and absolute truth. In fact, it is in the interest of our psychological development and social well-being that we begin with such an illusion. For some the illusion never fades, but for those who expose themselves to other cultures, historical epochs, and language communities the illusion begins to fade and we come into the freedom that is philosophy. Philosophy is, apart from all the high sounding definitions, the awareness and pursuit of a second truth that provides a better way to conceptualize our experience. The great example of this in our Western history is Socrates.

In the Platonic dialogues, Socrates is always showing his interlocutors that there is something wrong with their understanding. Not that Socrates has the right understanding—he seldom does—but he does have the right questions. The right questions are those that humble us and do violence to our inherited understanding in order to make us question what we think we know. By humbling us they open us to real learning and the realization that there is more to this world than we had imagined. Things are not simply given to us in experience; they are interpreted, and, for those who are on intellectual or spiritual journeys, there is always at least the hint that there is a better way to interpret what we are experiencing.

I've met a couple of Socrates types in my life, but they usually weren't in classrooms. One such Socrates was Mr. Miller. He was a retired Episcopal priest who would have lunch nearly every day at the restaurant where I tended bar. That's right: I was a bartender for eleven years while I was going to school. Mr. Miller was ninety-three at the time and I was a thirty-one year old bartender who had aspirations of becoming a philosopher. As soon as I saw him, I would make his scotch sour and bring it over to his table. Since he came in early before the lunch crowd, I would usually sit and talk for a few minutes. One day after talking with him, I remember remarking to Al, the other bartender, how smart Mr. Miller was. "Well," Al responded, "he's three times your age. When you get to be 93, you'll be that smart too." Even then, I knew that there was something wrong with that. It would be nice if we got smarter by getting older and simply acquiring more information, but intelligence is not simply a matter of acquiring information. Real intelligence is more a matter of assessing and altering the understanding through which we process the data of our experience. Critical thinking is not a matter of accepting what conforms to our understanding and rejecting what does not conform. Many people conceive of critical thinking in just such a simplistic way, but that is to make our understanding sacred and the measure by which we judge all things. Sacred truth, however, is greater than our understanding and should have the power to change the way we conceptualize our experience. This is what lies at the base of philosophical thinking. It is the ability to allow select data to alter our understanding in order to create new interpretations.

On one occasion when I brought Mr. Miller his drink and sat with him for a moment, he commented on how strange it was that in almost every Indo-European language the word for the first numerical digit is always pronounced with an *un* or *ien* sound. I immediately responded by commenting that wasn't true in English where *one* doesn't sound anything like that—to which Miller took out a pen and wrote on his newspaper, O-N-E. He asked, "How do you pronounce that?" I thought this must be where the O is pronounced like a W, as in words like _____? Where is an O ever pronounced like a W?

It is very natural to accept as true what we learn as children. We all begin there, but to hold those things as sacred truths throughout our lives is to deny other forms of intelligence. Indeed, the kind of intelligence that has caused our human condition to advance begins by our questioning of the way we have been taught to conceptualize things and setting out in search of a better perspective through which to organize and make sense of our experience. Our intellectual and spiritual development may begin with an elementary stage where we simply accept and learn to apply the conceptual understanding that we receive largely through language acquisition. Our early educational experiences are all about accepting the way our culture, history, and language communities teach us to interpret the world. If we do it quickly and accurately we are labeled smart, but that is only the first stage in our intellectual development. The second stage is quite different and begins when we come to question that inherited understanding. It is a second stage and we certainly cannot start there. We all need some type of foundation that purports to be true from which to begin, but that understanding must eventually be seen as provisional if we are ever to pursue an authentic intellectual or spiritual life. Sadly, many want nothing to do with such a life. What they want from science or religion is certainty and the sense of security that comes with the belief that *we know*. This is most natural and the basis for our early development. Psychological research bears this out. When children under a certain age are taught the rules of a particular game, and then later told that the rules are going to be changed, their response is that you can't change the rules—the rules are the rules and not open to change.

Change must be a terrifying thing to a child. Indeed, it continues to terrify many adults, so much so that many insist that their understanding is not provisional at all but certain and absolute. They make their initial understanding the sacred anchor which provides that secure feeling—that sense that they know how things work. Such people may say that they have faith, but it is faith in their own inherited understanding and not a faith in something greater than themselves. They shrink back from any real intellectual or spiritual journey and are content with the false security of what they were taught. Aldous Huxley describes it beautifully when he says,

> Every individual is at once the beneficiary and the
> victim of the linguistic tradition into which he has
> been born—the beneficiary inasmuch as language
> gives access to the accumulated records of other
> people's experience, the victim insofar as it con-
> firms him in the belief that reduced awareness is
> the only awareness....[4]

I once heard someone say, "The reason we read a lot of books is so we don't believe what we learned at our mother's knee." Certainly, what we learned there was essential. It allowed us to function in the world, but its truth was the truth of the social conventions that hold society together. That initial understanding was never intended to answer life's big questions—the questions that we are not ready for until later in life. A soul has to age some before it is ready for the big questions, and some souls are never ready for those questions. Some remain young souls forever.

We live in a culture that tells us that it is good to be a young soul—to know what's going on, and to "have it all together," but that is the naiveté of the early years of life. Eventually, the truth of that initial understanding is shattered. Of course, we can, and many do, continue to hold to that truth in spite of all the evidence to the contrary. Others, however, set out on an intellectual and spiritual journey in pursuit of a greater truth. This journey is not for the quick and clever who

---

4.   Huxley. *The Doors of Perception.* 23.

purport to know everything, but for those who see how fragile their understanding is. It is not for those who are certain of what they know, but for those who, like Socrates, know that what they know is not to be trusted as sacred, and that the ultimate truth is always beyond us, beckoning us to follow.

Philosophy, as a discipline, is all about learning to think about things differently. It is not about acquiring more information but thinking about that information in different ways. Science may purport to be about the way the world is, but philosophy is about how we think about the world. History and human consciousness sometimes advance because we discover additional data about the world. The invention of the telescope and microscope, along with the discovery of the new world, were certainly of that nature. But civilization usually advances, not by discovering more data, but by discovering new ways to think about the data. Copernicus, Newton, Einstein, and Heidegger were philosophers who gave us new ways to think about the data of our experience.

Philosophical people often find themselves at the top of organizations because of their ability to see things through wider eyes than the rest of the herd. Just as often, however, they are labeled heretics and executed before others realize that they really did have a better way of seeing things. This should not be surprising. Those who pursue a second truth or better way to interpret their experience and are vocal about it, threaten the foundational understanding that so many others hold as the sacred truth from which they draw their sense of security. People with great security needs will always seek to silence the *differant* and the *avant-garde*. Both Socrates and Jesus offered us a better way to interpret our experience and both were killed for having done so.

CHAPTER TWO

Socrates, Descartes, and the Two Truths

SOCRATES WAS A GREAT historical figure, but the people of Athens 2,500 years ago were not prepared for him. Things have not changed. Most of us are not ready for a Socrates who might appear in our lives and threaten both our understanding and the false security that comes from believing that we know. The belief that our knowledge is certain provides a sense of security, albeit a false sense. When someone challenges what we think we know—when they take that sense of certainty from us—we most often respond unfavorably toward them. This was undeniably the case with the people of Athens and their response to Socrates. Yet, all real learning—the kind of learning that causes our understanding to develop over time, both as individuals and as a species—always requires that someone or something does violence to our current understanding. Real learning takes place only when we are forced to abandon the truth of our initial orientation that we uncritically acquired in our childhood. This is often especially challenging to those who obtained that initial orientation or understanding quickly and accurately and were thereby dubbed "the smart kids."

Socrates always has the most trouble with the smart kids, because they think they know how things work and take pride in that knowing. Real learning, however, at least the kind of which Socrates speaks, begins when we hesitate and question the understanding through which we have been taught to interpret the world. Thus, there are two very different types of learning, since there are two very different truths that we seek to know. The first truth is acquired uncritically, since young fragile selves have no basis from which to take a stand against everyone telling them that they know and want the young to know what they know. The second, philosophical truth of which Socrates speaks is far more mysterious. It is in fact a truth that we can never possess but only pursue. It possesses us, or at least those among us who seek a better way to understand our experience. We are ready for a second, philosophical truth when we realize that we do not objectively experience the world, other people, or God, but we interpret those experiences based upon the understanding we bring to them. Since we live in a time of human history where we have become aware of this interpretive nature of our human condition, we have entered a Socratic age, where we are freer than ever before to question the conventions and judgments through which we have been taught to interpret our experience. This freedom is not appreciated by everyone. With many people, it produces anxiety and even violent reactions.

Of course, there is a real world apart from our interpretation of it, but the great insight of our age is that we cannot get any closer to it than our interpreted experience of it. That does not mean, however, that our interpretation cannot improve.

Indeed, it can become a more transparent interpretation. In other words, we can change our understanding in order to eliminate bad interpretations. That seems to be what Socrates is always doing with his interlocutors. He is trying to convince them that there is something wrong with their understanding, but he never tells them what the right understanding is, and that is because he doesn't know. He says in the *Apology* that such "real wisdom is the property of God, and ... human wisdom has little or no value."[5] But if that is the case, why does Socrates spend his entire life pursuing a wisdom he can never possess? The answer is quite simple. Socrates is not interested in possessions. He has no possessions and neither does he see wisdom and knowledge as a possession the way we so easily do. We think of truth as the understanding we possess, but that is simply the first truth. The second truth that Socrates is always pursuing is not a possession but an end that creates a journey. Furthermore, Socrates comes to love that second truth, and the intellectual and spiritual journey it creates, so much so that he never wants it to end. It is this longing for a truth that provides a better way to understand and interpret our experience that fuels those who have entered into genuine intellectual or spiritual journeys. What Socrates longs for is a better perspectival understanding that will reveal still more of what he is encountering in his experience. Unlike others who set out on such a journey but all too quickly imagine that they have reached the end and now have truth firmly in their grasp, Socrates is not so naive. He is comfortable with the longing in a way that most of us seldom are. Most of us want to get

---

5. Plato. *Apology*. 23a3-9.

beyond the longing, and we do that by longing for things that we can attain and thereby rid ourselves of that feeling that we do not have what we want.

The kind of truth that Socrates is pursuing is never fully realized. Socrates may want to know as God knows, but he is not so naïve to believe that he can attain that. He knows it is something we long for and that is enough to satisfy him. To really live a contented life—the kind of life that Socrates reveals—we have to be satisfied with the longing. We have to love the journey and never want it to end. Knowing as God knows will always be out of reach and that is a good thing, since it is the longing after that and not its attainment that is meant to satisfy us. If we allow the longing after that divine truth to possess us, we, like Socrates, rise above the disappointment that always follows our longing for lesser things, whether we attain them or not. Socrates knew that the only thing that can really satisfy us is this great longing. Our sin is that we want the longing to stop so we create petty distractions that we can possess and hopefully feel satisfied by possessing them.

Our first truth was one of those possessions. It was a truth that we needed to possess in order to have some orientation to the world, but perhaps that is what it means to be born in sin. We are born with a nature that very quickly comes to think that we know truth as God knows truth.[6] It is natural for us to believe that lie, since, as we have said, it is essential to our early psychological health that we embrace our initial orientation to the world as *the* truth. Our redemption begins when we start to see

---

6.   Genesis 3:5.

the conventional nature of that truth. Unfortunately, when we set out in search of a second truth, we all too easily imagine that it must be like our first truth: a truth that we possess in order to be able to rightly interpret the data of our experience. Any such pseudo-second truth, however, will be mythic and clouded in a lie similar to our foundational truth, although it might for a time give us a better interpretation. The only truth that is not mythic is the kind of mystical truth that is the object of Socrates' journey. That, by the way, is the only kind of truth that is *scientific* as well.

Real science is always open and never closed the way our foundational truth is closed and held as certain. Scientific truth is always open to revision in a way that Socrates' truth is always being questioned and critiqued. This is not the truth of the Platonic forms that have always been associated with Plato and Socrates, but a truth about the human condition. It is the truth that Socrates says makes us, "better, braver, and more active men,"[7] because we constantly seek a better way to understand and interpret our experience. That better understanding is always out in front and never in our possession, but it is the mystical quality of truth that draws us to seek ever new perspectives through which to interpret our world, ourselves, other people, and God.

This is the truth that is at the base of the Socratic Method. It may begin with our admission of ignorance in order that learning might go forth, but it also involves a very different concept of truth than the truth to which we were initially exposed. Initially, we were told how everyone else understood things, but Socrates

---

7.   Plato. *Meno*. 86b5-c2.

was never content with such a common understanding. He was never interested in how most people conceptualize their experience, but was always looking for a better conceptualization. He believed that if we had a better understanding of courage, love, and virtue that we would be more courageous, loving, and virtuous. Likewise, he believed that everyone seeks the good life but few find it because most do not have a sufficient concept of what would constitute the good life.[8] Thus, people get, or at least increase their chances of getting, courage, love, virtue, and the good life by having a better concept of such things.

What seems to have irritated so many people that Socrates came in contact with was not that he showed them that the concepts they had inherited were insufficient, but that he almost never offered a better concept. Those who had trouble with Socrates assumed that he must have had the right conceptual understanding, since he knew that their conceptual understanding was wrong and could demonstrate how erroneous it was. The way a Socratic dialogue usually unfolds is with Socrates inquiring into a particular area with an interlocutor, whom he questions concerning their understanding of some concept like courage, virtue, or love. After the interlocutor has made several failed attempts at explaining their concept, they surrender to Socrates and concede that they do not know and ask for the right understanding from him. But Socrates is dissatisfied with his own understanding as well. The people of Athens seem to have been unable to forgive Socrates for this. They could have tolerated Socrates if, after he had destroyed their foundational

---

8.   Plato. *Meno*. 77b2-78c4.

understanding, he had provided another understanding even more solid and certain than what he had destroyed, but he seldom did. Even when he does, and when the interlocutor is impressed with the new understanding, we get the sense that Socrates is still in search of something more.

That is not what we want from Socrates. If he destroys our inherited understanding, we demand that he replace it with *the* right understanding. In fact, since Plato's Socrates speaks of a world of immutable and eternal forms, we anticipate that, after he has debunked our concepts and shown them to be insufficient, he will reveal to us the true form or concept. We imagine that must be his purpose in showing us how insufficient our concepts are, and at times in the dialogues it might appear that way, but that is seldom the case. The reason for this is that Socrates believes that real truth always eludes us. The truth beckons and calls us to itself, but is always beyond our grasp. It is the *al di la* that speaks to us and tells us there is a better way to understand and interpret what we are experiencing, but it is never fully realized and we are always left in that discontent. It is that discontent, however, that Socrates and all real seekers of truth seem to love. Indeed, it is this strange discontent that Socrates says makes us "better, braver, and more active men,"[9] who are always looking to learn of a better way to conceptualize things. It is the truth that speaks to Copernicus and Einstein and tells them to think about what they are considering differently.

This truth is certainly different from the conventional truth with which we all begin. Furthermore, while everyone

---

9. Ibid.

experiences the truth of our foundational understanding, many people never move beyond that initial understanding in search of a second truth. In fact, many people would never recognize such a thing as truth at all, since their idea of truth is something they could possess and therein feel certain and secure. A truth that calls them to a journey into the unknown is frightening, and as Socrates says is only for those braver souls who are willing to pursue something they will never ultimately possess. This is what lies at the base of the Socratic discourse and what is behind all genuine philosophical or spiritual inquiry. Unfortunately, we always want the journey to end where we began, with an absolute certainty that can serve as a concrete foundation for what we know, but that is never what Socrates offers.

Even on those occasions where Socrates does appear to give us something solid in the way of knowledge, and the interlocutor is impressed with what Socrates has delivered, Socrates never really embraces it as an end. There is a great example of this in the *Meno*. Meno has questioned whether we can ever really learn anything since if we don't know what we are looking for, we would not know it even if we found it; and if we do know what we are looking for, we would not need to look for it, but would already have that knowledge. Socrates' answer to this learning paradox is what has come to be known as the famous recollection myth, in which he explains that we existed before this life and had actually seen the eternal forms in our previous existence. Therefore, learning is not really about learning things anew, but remembering or recognizing in the things of this world their resemblance to the eternal forms that we had experienced in our previous existence. Meno is enormously impressed, and claims that Socrates has just proven the immortality of the soul, since we do seem to learn things and Socrates' myth has just explained how that is possible. Socrates has just provided Meno with an understanding through which he might interpret and make sense of the experience of learning. Socrates, on the other hand, is not so easily impressed. He responds by saying that he doesn't know if he would fight over that, or as other translations have it, that he wouldn't swear an oath to attest to the truth of that story. He does say, however, that he is willing to swear an oath or fight over the fact that we will be better and braver human beings if we pursue learning rather than shrinking back from it.[10]

Interestingly, the truth that is at the base of Socrates' intellectual journey is nothing like the foundational truths that religion or science provide. It is a mysterious truth that tells those who pursue it that there is a better way to understand what they are trying to know. For Socrates, or anyone else who embarks on an intellectual or spiritual journey, knowledge is always provisional. Socrates always imagines that there is a better understanding and although it might be reserved for God alone, it is always worthwhile to pursue that better understanding, if for no other reason than if you don't, you will all too easily come to think that your present understanding and God's understanding are the same. That seems to be the most dangerous of positions. We see the effects of such fundamentalisms in the world today, and it was that same fundamentalism that killed Socrates. He

---

10. Plato. *Meno.* 86b4-c1

revealed to the Athenians that their understanding was not as sacred as they had thought. That was the real "crime" for which he was killed. True, Socrates believed that there was perfect knowledge and we were even given a glimpse of it with geometry. We know that a circle is a figure whose every point is equidistant from its center, and it seems that Socrates thought that if all of our concepts were as clear and distinct as that, we would have the kind of certain and precise knowledge that would be ideal. What is revealed throughout the Platonic discourses, however, is that we never arrive at such knowledge. We are never at the end of this dialogue in pursuit of truth, but Socrates thinks that the pursuit of a truth that always eludes us has a humbling effect that makes learning possible. What prevents learning is the belief that we already have the best possible understanding. The truth that there is always a better way to conceptualize what we are experiencing is this mysterious second truth that is infinitely knowable, and therefore there is no end to our pursuit of it.

Unlike Socrates, however, there have always been those who claim to have reached the end of the journey and possess the last word. This is never scientific, since real science is always open and never closed. It is, however, very hard to live in that liminal space of not knowing, and therefore there is a psychological tendency to imagine that our present understanding is not provisional at all but ultimate truth. If we remain in our infancy, all truth is treated like our initial truth and held to be certain, but that is a very different notion of truth than what Socrates calls us to follow.

The Modern Period and the Suppression of Socratic Truth

Modern fundamentalism is antithetical to the kind of truth to which Socrates calls us. Its philosophical origins can be traced to the early modern period and the advent of modern materialism. In the late medieval world, anomalies had begun to appear in the Aristotelian understanding that had dominated the medieval world. Developments within the 16th century presented us with data that the Aristotelian understanding had not anticipated. New worlds had been discovered of which Aristotle was unaware. The discovery of civilizations west of the great sea meant the world was much bigger than Aristotle had imagined. Likewise, the inventions of the telescope and microscope at the beginning of the 17th century added dimensions to the world that exceeded the Aristotelian scope. The biggest change, however, that signaled the death knell of Aristotle was the advent of what was termed "the corpuscular philosophy."

Many of the great 17th century thinkers (e.g., Descartes, Locke, Galileo, Newton, Boyle, etc.) were adherents of "the corpuscular philosophy." It maintained that what created the sensible perceptions that make up the world of our experience were tiny insensible corpuscles (later dubbed "atoms"). These corpuscles were made up of primary qualities or pure matter. The only qualities that these corpuscles or atoms possessed were extension, figure, solidity, number, and motion. Consequently, other, secondary qualities like smells, colors, tastes, or sounds do not exist in the same way as do the primary qualities that make up the corpuscles or atoms. These secondary qualities, however, are merely sensations within us caused by the shape, arrangement, and motion of the primary qualities that make up the corpuscles.[11]

The great advantage that corpuscular philosophy offered over that of Aristotle was that it allowed for a mathematical physics in a way that Aristotle thought was impossible. According to Aristotle, the natural world was made up of many different forms or natural species. Trees had a different form and were therefore of a different species (or kind of thing) from rocks or squirrels. Aristotle even believed that we had been equipped with an active or agent intellect that gave us the ability to know these natural forms. Thomas Aquinas, who translated Aristotle into medieval Christian terms, argued that God was not a deceiver and would not have placed us in this world without equipping us with a sufficient knowledge of it. Part of that natural equipping involved an ability to know how God had organized the world into different forms or species.

Corpuscular philosophy certainly undermined that view. If God had equipped us with an active intellect to know the Aristotelian forms, he really did deceive us, since corpuscular philosophy held that the way God had actually organized the world was not through Aristotelian forms but through corpuscular structures. Several pieces of gold were not members of the same species or kind of thing we call gold because they shared an Aristotelian form but because they all had the same atomic structure, Au79. Likewise, different bodies of water do not

---

11. Locke. *Essay*, IV. iii. 11-16.

share the same Aristotelian form, but rather the same molecular structure, H_2O.

With the Aristotelian forms, a mathematical physics was impossible. Mathematics only works when we have only one kind of thing. We can only add, subtract, multiple, or divide when we have all members of the same species: three apples plus four apples equals seven apples, but three pears plus four peaches cannot be quantified. Mathematics works within forms but not between different forms as was necessary when dealing with nature, or so Aristotle thought. Of course, what the corpuscularians said was that everything was the same kind of thing, namely matter. It may appear that there are different kinds of things, as Aristotle had thought, but ultimately everything is reduced to mere matter, and matter only differs in quantity and not quality. For the corpuscular philosophy and later the atomic chemistry that grew out of it, all matter is the same and what differentiates gold from hydrogen is that the one has a different quantity of electrons and protons than the other, but all the protons and electrons are the same kind of thing. Since all electrons and protons are of the same form or a mere composite of primary qualities, and the only difference between a hydrogen atom and a gold atom is that one has more or fewer electrons and protons than the other, they differ only in quantity. If gold simply had more of the same basic matter than hydrogen, then perhaps a purely quantitative or mathematical understanding of the world would be possible.

Having reduced all of nature to a single form (matter), modern thinkers took a huge step toward establishing a mathematical physics, but even with that step taken there remained yet another problem: how could we be certain that the new science was truly replicating nature? Aristotle, and nearly everyone else up until the modern period, believed that a true science of nature would have to guarantee a match between our understanding of nature and nature itself, but what could possibly give us such a guarantee?

Medieval thinkers had found such a guarantee in their theology and the idea that God was not a deceiver. If God had given us our empirical senses and God was not a deceiver, then our senses could be trusted and what appeared to be the nature of things was, indeed, the way things truly were. That worked with Aristotle's physics but not with the new corpuscular philosophy. According to corpuscular philosophy, God had not equipped us with senses capable of knowing the truth of the natural world, since our senses did not have access to the essential material elements (atoms) by which the world was actually organized. In the modern period, Copernicus also contributed to the idea that our God-given senses were not to be trusted, since the sun does not go around the earth each day as it appears.

If our senses could no longer be trusted, we would need some other basis for guaranteeing that our understanding of the world was in fact true. One option was to believe that God had adequately equipped us, but it was *reason* rather than our empirical senses that we should trust as the means God had intended us to utilize. Reason, after the model of mathematics, was what made us different from the rest of the animal kingdom, and it would be reason that would bring us to a proper knowledge of this world. Some even believed that it was reason that most closely linked us to the divine.

Another option was to believe that God did little more than create the world and now it was up to us to figure out how best to live in it. This was an easy option for the deists and later for atheists who would no longer be interested in trying to figure out how God actually ordered the world. They would no longer seek to replicate God's understanding but rather would create an understanding for themselves; that is, an understanding of the natural world that best suited our human purposes. The problem was a little different for theists who wanted to maintain that God had equipped us to know the world as He had created it, but the way He had equipped us was with the kind of reason we find in mathematics rather than an Aristotelian active intellect. Thus, both atheists and theists looked to reason. The question was how to proceed. What was needed was a method that would join the kind of thinking we find in mathematics with the study of nature. The French philosopher and mathematician Rene Descartes (1596-1650) provided just such a method. He is often called the father of modern philosophy.

Descartes

In his *Discourse on Method*, Descartes suggests a method of reasoning that would have an enormous effect upon shaping the thinking of the modern mind. The purpose of his method was to establish foundations for human knowledge that were as certain as the truths of mathematics. Descartes thought that mathematics was certain because of a method of reasoning that was unlike the methods of other disciplines. This method, which he claimed to be at work in mathematics, was one which began by accepting "nothing as true which [was] . . . not clearly recognized to be so."[12] Descartes says that we should "avoid . . . any prejudice in judgments, to accept in them nothing more than what was presented to [the] mind so clearly and distinctly that [we] could have no occasion to doubt it."[13]

Paradoxically, by attempting to eliminate "any prejudice," Descartes was laying the foundation for one of the major prejudices at the root of modern thinking. That is, that it was possible to have a point of view that was not a view from a particular point. He, and the modern thinkers that followed him, believed that an unbiased view was both ideal and possible. Descartes, and the modern thinkers that inherited his legacy, saw mathematics, and the kind of thinking that it employed, as such an unbiased view. The fact that it admitted only ideas that were so "clear and distinct" that it was impossible to doubt them meant that such ideas were certain and therefore true. What made the kind of thinking we find in a mathematical science like geometry different from our thinking in other disciplines was that it began with unshakable truths. The fact that a triangle cannot be anything but the sum of two right angles or that a circle cannot be anything but a figure whose every point is equidistant from the center meant that geometry was founded upon a certainty that was absent in other disciplines. The Cartesian ambition was

---

12. Descartes. *Discourse on Method.* 92.
13. Ibid.

that if we based a science of nature on such a model, it would provide a kind of certainty that would overcome the vast variety of opinions that had plagued previous attempts at creating a science of nature. He imagined that if we based the new science upon the kind of method he suggested, it would put an end to any "prejudice in judgments."[14]

Of course, if we were to accept *only* those things of which we could be certain, the senses would no longer be a reliable source of truth, since our senses cannot provide clear and distinct ideas that are certain and beyond doubt. This represented a huge break from medieval thinking, which trusted the senses on the theological basis that God was not a deceiver. Descartes was acutely aware that this could put him in trouble with the church. The church of the Inquisition dealt severely with anything they considered heresy, as Galileo (1564-1642) had discovered. Descartes was aware of Galileo's situation and was careful to avoid a similar fate for himself. Throughout his writings, he went to great lengths to avoid offending the church. He knew that his support of the corpuscular philosophy put him at odds with the Aristotelian teachings of the church, so he paid homage to God and the church throughout his writings. If accused of heresy, he could argue that, although he was rejecting the Aristotelian idea of an active intellect and that basis for our conceptualization of the world, God did equip us to know truth. Indeed, He had given us something better than an active intellect by giving us the kind of reasoning we find in mathematics.

---

14. Ibid.

His method, and the philosophy that flows from it, begins where all attempts at knowledge begin—with a noble lie. Socrates had done the same thing. Socrates told a myth about how learning was possible because of our experience of the forms in a previous life, but he quickly admits that he is not willing to swear an oath concerning the truth of that myth. The truth to which he is willing to swear an oath, however, is that we will be better and braver human beings if we pursue learning.[15] Since most of us are not willing to pursue learning unless we believe that we can arrive at truth, a noble lie is necessary.

Descartes makes the same start. He begins with the noble lie that all clear and distinct ideas are true, but clear and distinct ideas are no more than clear and distinct ideas. All unicorns have one horn is as clear and distinct an idea as all bachelors are unmarried men. Both are beyond doubt but no more than the association of ideas. To define truth in such a way is a huge leap, but it is a necessary leap. We must begin somewhere and Descartes decides to begin by equating clear and distinct ideas with truth simply because clear and distinct ideas are beyond doubt and what is not able to be doubted must be true.

By defining truth as that which is beyond doubt, Descartes was able to build up a body of clear and distinct ideas simply by finding ideas that were not open to doubt. His method was simply to doubt everything and when he found things that could not be doubted he dubbed them true. He claimed to begin with the idea that his mind exists (*Cogito ergo sum*—I think therefore I am), because when he tried to doubt the existence of his own

---

15. Plato. *Meno*. 86b4-86c2.

mind, he found that the very act of doubting his mind confirmed its existence (*Dubito ergo sum*—I doubt therefore I am).

He claimed this is his starting point and the rock-solid foundation from which he begins, but the real foundation for his philosophy is presented in the section of his *Discourse on Method* that immediately precedes the section on the *cogito*. There he presents the moral rules derived from his method the second maxim of which he says is to act as if he knows even when he doesn't (that's my paraphrase). What he actually says is, "My second maxim was that of being as firm and resolute in my actions as I could be, and not to follow less faithfully opinions the most dubious, when my mind was once made up regarding them, than if these had been beyond doubt."[16] He goes on to use the example of being lost in a forest and not knowing the way out. He says what is best and "very true and very certain"[17] is that we should pick a direction and follow it resolutely without wavering; that is, we should act as if we know even when we don't. Without that conviction and the resolute action to follow it, we will wander aimlessly. So we need a conviction or belief to get started. This is much like Socrates' belief that we will be better and braver human beings for believing a certain myth in order to get us started. There is nothing wrong with this approach and in fact it is essential to any intellectual or spiritual journey. We must begin with a foundational truth and act like we know, or can know, in order to get started.

The great difference between Socrates and Descartes is that

---

16. Descartes. *Discourse on Method*. 96.
17. Ibid.

the one gives us a myth to *start* us on a journey, while the other gives us a myth that purports to *end* our long journey. It is easy to see Socrates' initial myth as a starting point for a journey into truth, and maybe that is how we should understand Descartes as well, but the problem with Descartes is that what he presents as truth ends the journey before it begins. By claiming that all clear and distinct ideas are true he truncates the notion of truth to something narrow and artificial. Descartes' truth is nothing like what we actually experience. Of course, if we are looking to reinforce our foundations in order that we never have to go on a journey in pursuit of a great truth, Descartes' notion has a great appeal. For those who have excessive needs for security and control, Descartes' truncated notion of truth is very attractive. It gives us a truth that we can possess and a feeling of confidence in our possession of it, but it leaves us in an abstract world whose truth is no more than the mere association of limited ideas and very different from the world we actually experience.

Descartes' truth gives us the illusion that our foundations can be certain, but in fact such a foundation is simply a faith in thinking about things in a certain way. It is a matter of shoring up our understanding in order to have it pass for truth but, as we have said, the second truth that we long for is always greater than our understanding. The only certainty we ever achieve in ourselves and our own understanding is to act like we know even when we don't. We are lost in the woods and it is necessary that we act like we know our way out even when we don't, but we need to recognize that we are acting out of faith rather than knowing.

Our foundations are always foundations of faith. This is the conclusion of Plato's *Theaetetus*. There Socrates and Theaetetus are trying to come to an understanding (definition) of knowledge. After several failed attempts they settle on the idea that knowledge is true opinion plus a *logos:* that is, a true opinion plus a reasoned account that supports that true opinion. That is still the definition of knowledge that many use today, but Socrates reminds us that it ultimately doesn't work because when we unpack our knowledge all the way back to the starting points, we come to words, and even before that letters for which there can be no *logos* or reasoned account. Why is it true that the letter L is the letter L? There is no reasoned account or *logos* to support that. It is just a convention that we accept in order to get started. This is always the case. When we trace things back to their foundations and look for a reasoned account to support them, we find nothing but the fact that we need to start somewhere, and we will be better and braver human beings for having acted as if we can know what we don't know.[18]

The Logical Positivists of the 20th century provide a great example of this. They were the philosophers who demanded verification of truth claims and stated their belief that: "We will accept nothing as meaningful unless it can be verified or falsified in observation." Of course, that statement is self-referentially false or meaningless by its own criterion. The statement cannot be verified or falsified in observation. It is a faith statement like all foundational beliefs. Descartes' foundations are the same. He puts his faith in clear and distinct ideas because he must put his

---

18. Plato. *Meno.* 86b:6-10.

faith in something if he has any hope of getting out of the forest in which he finds himself lost.

Certainly there is truth in what Descartes says. His first principle of acting like we know even when we don't know is absolutely true and the place from which we all begin. When lost in the forest, we should act as if we know even when we don't. This is in fact where we all begin, by believing that what we learn at our mother's knee is true, but for those who eventually set out on an intellectual or spiritual journey it always turns out to have been a provisional truth, which allowed us to get the inquiry into truth started.

Civilization has gone forth because certain individuals saw anomalies in their initial orientation and set out in search of a better way to interpret their experience. Certainly they began with the truth of their inherited understanding, but the truth they sought was beyond them and not something they possessed. Socrates is the great example of this, but few of us are like Socrates. Most of us, even when we do set out on an intellectual or spiritual journey, are all too quick to dub whatever better understanding we come to at the next turn: *the truth*, but that is to close our mind to the truth of an ever better perspective that is always beyond us and beckoning us to follow. Descartes may have led us into a truth that fortifies our own understanding, but the journey leads us into a truth that is always greater than our understanding. Sadly, we live in a world that is largely Cartesian rather than Socratic, and we worship our own understanding rather than something greater than our own understanding.

This is the real spiritual divide in the world today. There

are those who worship their own understanding as the only truth and kill others who do not see that understanding as sacred, and there are others, be they Christians, Muslims, or Jews, who are spiritually mature and worship a truth that is greater than their own understanding. The spiritually immature are those who kill Socrates in whatever age he appears because he challenges the understanding they hold as sacred. Healthy, mature spirituality and religion, however, are like healthy science: ever open to a greater understanding. Unfortunately, we are not ready for a journey into such a truth until a certain age, and some are never ready. Some remain young souls forever and are never ready for a greater truth that humbles them; instead, they cling desperately to the mythic certainty of their own understanding.

Of course, the real trick is to honor our foundational truths and hold onto them since they are the basis for our interaction with others, but at the same time never hold them so tightly that we refuse to acknowledge that other truth that beckons to us from beyond. Both truths are essential and there is a dance that we do between the two. The sad part is that we keep thinking that we have to choose between the two, since there is only one truth, but in terms of the understanding through which human beings interpret their experience there are two truths between which we must learn to live.

We have a better chance of that today, since the 19th and 20th centuries have brought us to a better perspective of truth than what Descartes offered with his truncated, early modern view. Descartes' concept of truth provided us with the kind of certainty from which we need to begin but that is only one truth concerning our human condition. More recent philosophers like William James,[19] Alfred North Whitehead,[20] Martin Heidegger,[21] Ludwig Wittgenstein,[22] and Hans Georg Gadamer[23] have pointed us toward a second truth that is always greater than our understanding but very much a part of our human experience.

---

19. *The Will to Believe* (1897).
20. *The Concept of Nature* (1920).
21. *Being and Time* (1927).
22. *Philosophical Investigations* (1953).
23. *Truth and Method* (1960).

CHAPTER THREE

Jesus and the Spiritual Journey

THE SPIRITUAL JOURNEY of which Jesus speaks follows the same form as the intellectual journey that Socrates calls philosophy. That should not be too surprising since there are many similarities between Jesus and Socrates. To begin with they both had trouble with the conventionally smart guys. The religious leaders of Jesus' day were confident in their own understanding and equated it with truth, just as the leaders of Athenian society believed they had the truth. Socrates and Jesus both got into trouble because they spoke of a truth that was greater than the truth that was possessed by people in positions of power. People with great security needs want a truth that they can possess and feel confident in possessing, but Socrates and Jesus present us with a greater truth that cannot be possessed but only sought.

Like the rest of us, both Socrates and Jesus begin where we all begin with a foundational truth that we inherit from our history, culture, and language community. They were given an understanding that allowed them to interpret the world in a very similar way to everyone else in their community. Some of us retain that foundational understanding as our only perspective all of our lives; others, however, come to see things in a different light. Socrates and Jesus are certainly examples of individuals who came to a better way to conceptualize and interpret their experience, but many of us do a similar thing at least in some area of our lives. Some of us come to a new perspective in the area of business, sports, science, theology, or even our personal relationships. This is simply because the things we love, we wish to know better and knowing something better does not always mean that we simply get more information about that thing. Often we come to know something better by coming to think about it differently. In other words, we come to know something better by seeking a second truth or better way to understand and interpret that thing. This is the divine truth of which both Socrates and Jesus speak.

The journey in pursuit of such a divine truth is always a matter of leaving the familiar and moving into an unknown land where our foundational orientation is no longer capable of giving us the security and certainty it once did. Abraham, Moses, and Buddha all set out on journeys. They were called out and away from what they knew, because when we think we know real learning is impossible unless it is more than uncritically accepting what conforms to our understanding and rejecting what does not conform. If we are to encounter a more divine truth it must be in something like a wilderness place where all of our cultural and linguistic filters that made quick sense of our experience are no longer viable. That is the nature of a spiritual journey just as it is the nature of an intellectual journey. The old understanding which insists that the data must conform to it must break down in order for us to simply behold that which is beyond our understanding.

What is beyond our understanding is frightening and often we are desperate to make sense of the unfamiliar data. The Biblical revelation is full of stories about people having experiences with the unfamiliar angelic beings whose address is always "Fear not" or "Do not be afraid."[24] The fear that unfamiliar settings produce can make us desperate for some way to make sense of the experience, but the revelation from the divine messenger is always to wait and not be afraid. Don't be so quick to escape that unknowing and jump at the first understanding that makes sense of the experience.

The Jesus story begins with Jesus being brought into the wilderness and fasting for forty days. The wilderness is not simply a fast from food but equally a fast from the understanding that our culture and language community had provided. Our human conventions don't apply in the wilderness and we are left alone with unfamiliar data. In the wilderness all of the social conventions by which we were taught to interpret our human world are no longer in play, and we learn to simply behold.[25] The experience of new terrain without a ready-made understanding to interpret it gives the data of our experience more authority than when an understanding is firmly in place. In the wilderness, Jesus opens himself to the pure unfiltered awe of the Divine presence, out of which a new understanding begins to

---

24. In the King James Version, "fear not" is mentioned 74, and "be not afraid" 29 times. In the New American Standard Bible, "fear not" appears 4 times, "do not fear" 57 times, and "do not be afraid" 46 times.

25. For more on the idea of beholding see, Maggie Ross, *Writing the Icon of the Heart: in Silence Beholding*.

form. This is the nature of the journey which Jesus models and calls us to follow. He tells us repeatedly throughout the Gospels, "Follow me."[26] I take that as an idiom for "do what I do" and the first thing that Jesus did was to go into the wilderness where, without all the filters that normally sift and sort the data of our experience, we encounter data with wonder rather than understanding. This is the essence of a spiritual and intellectual life that is more than a trust and faith in our own understanding. Most of us do not choose such a life and prefer to stay at home with those truths that we share with everyone else rather than to enter a journey into the unknown. Most Christians much prefer to establish a Christian tradition, upon the one time, in one Gospel, Jesus says late at night to one person, "You must be born again,"[27] rather than the seventeen times Jesus says "follow me." There seem to be more "Born Again" Christians than there are "Follow Me" Christians. Certainly, there is nothing wrong with being "born again" but the idea of a new birth is just the start of a journey rather than the acquisition of some ultimate truth that ends the journey.

Sadly, most are not interested in a Jesus who calls them to a journey into the unknown. What most want is an understanding of the Jesus message that assures them that they are going to heaven. This is the Jesus that sells so well to religious people, but a much better reading of the Jesus message is that

26. Matthew 4:19; 8:22; 9:9; 16:24; 19:21; Mark 2:14; 8:34; 10:21; Luke 5:27; 9:23, 59; 18:22;John 1:43; 10:27; 12:26; 13:36; 21:19.
27. John 3:7. NIV.

he is calling us to a spiritual journey, just as Socrates calls us to an intellectual journey. Jesus' journey begins with his embrace of the Jewish culture into which he was born. Just as Socrates acknowledges and is thankful for the Athenian culture which provided a foundation without which his later inquiry would be impossible,[28] Jesus does the same. We don't know at what specific point Socrates set out in search of a greater truth than what he had inherited, but there is the account of a forty day desert experience with Jesus. In such a wilderness the conventional understanding that we were told was sacred begins to fade, and we are opened to an experience of pure beholding. It is the experience of the divine outside the boundaries of our limited understanding. Such an experience reopens us to the mystery that our culture, history, and language community tried to eliminate with our initial orientation. It brings us to the realization that our experience is much bigger than our understanding, and the possibility of a new and authentic second truth opens before us. In the wilderness our understanding expands to take in the divine mystery rather than eliminate it.

Like modern science, modern theology was intent upon eliminating mystery, but the spiritual journey is all about entering into the mystery. Jesus' teachings are never about giving us answers that will end the journey, but rather about offering a perspective or understanding that will allow us to follow him into the mystery of the Divine. Unfortunately, almost all versions of Christianity have made his teachings into the kind of foundational truth that represent our initial understanding rather

---

28. Plato. *Apology.* 50e2-51c6.

than the second truth that is the object of a spiritual journey. There is nothing wrong with having an initial, common understanding of Jesus and the Gospel, but as we become aware of a second truth or better conceptual perspective for ourselves, we should begin to realize that what Jesus is revealing in the Gospels is his own unique second truth.

Modern scholarship was for the most part unaware of this. Modern scholars told us that if we wanted to find the meaning in an ancient text we needed to study it in its original language, and there is something right about that, but it supposes that Jesus' concepts were the same as those of his language community. Of course, some of them were, but many of his concepts were unique to his authentic spiritual journey. This is always the case with those authentic individuals who advance civilization and human consciousness. Philosophers like Copernicus, Newton, and Einstein[29] did not discover new data but new ways to conceptualize the data. Philosophers are people who interpret their experience using their own unique understanding rather than their inherited perspective. The Irish philosopher George Berkeley (1685-1753) had very different concepts of things like "matter" or "ideas," just as Hegel (1770-1831) had a different concept of history. The same is true concerning great spiritual teachers, who like philosophers, re-conceptualize the concepts pertinent to their particular journey. Of course, most of these spiritual teachers, like the philosophers, wrote long books

---

29.   Such men were considered philosophers in their day and should be in our day as well since they did what is really at the base of all of philosophy; that is, they re-conceptualized of their experience.

explaining their new concepts and the view it produced. Jesus, however, never wrote such a book, but from the examples he gives of such things as faith, sin, love, mercy, and righteousness he clearly has very different concepts of such things than those of his language community or of ours. His concepts of such things are not common but personal and the result of his unique experience.

Foundational truths are not personal truths. They represent the truth of the common understanding that we all need to share in order to function socially. It is so common that we don't even think of it as a perspective or understanding but as objective truth since it seems to be held by everyone. Great spiritual teachers, however, do not offer a common understanding but rather the unique, personal understanding that has come out of their unique and authentic spiritual journeys. What the teachings of Jesus ultimately offer is not merely a foundational truth for later generations, but a conceptual perspective for anyone on a spiritual journey in pursuit of an authentic second truth.

Thus, the two truths of our human condition play out spiritually the same way they play out intellectually. Jesus was in pursuit of a second truth or better way to understand and interpret his experiences in the presence of the Divine. That second truth got translated into part of the common, foundational understanding that we inherit as part of our Western civilization, but it began as Jesus' personal conceptual understanding. Just as Socrates pursued his own unique conceptual understanding, so too Jesus had come to an authentic conceptual understanding that better reflected his experiences with the Divine than the understanding he had inherited.

Many of us may consider our inherited conceptual understanding as "Christian" but that understanding is very different from Jesus' second truth, which is the Jesus perspective. This second truth does not pretend to be objective, as does our inherited Christian understanding. It is not about the way things are apart from our understanding but rather the unique and personal understanding through which Jesus interpreted his spiritual journey. Just as Socrates gives us the truth of a perspective as a model for our own intellectual journey, Jesus offers us his perspective as a model for us to follow in our spiritual journey. This second truth that both Socrates and Jesus offer is only for those who are willing to leave the safe harbor of their foundational understanding and go on the kind of journey to which both Socrates and Jesus call us.

In order to do so, however, we need what Jesus calls great faith, since we are no longer clinging to what we know but pursuing the hope of a better understanding. Great faith, as Jesus understood, it had nothing to do with what we consider religious faith today. Our common understanding of religious faith is an unwavering belief in certain religious doctrines or teachings, but that is very different from what Jesus is talking about. In the only two instances where Jesus says that someone has great faith, neither has to do with those individuals having the right foundational beliefs. Neither of them are Jews or religious insiders possessing what would have been considered good theology in Jesus' day, but both had sensed that there was something greater than their own understanding at work in their lives.

From her personal experience the Canaanite woman knew that God takes care of even the dogs, and she refutes Jesus when he tells her that it is not right to give the children's bread to dogs.

And behold, a Canaanite woman from that region came out and cried, "Have mercy on me, O Lord, Son of David; my daughter is severely possessed by a demon." But he did not answer her a word. And his disciples came and begged him, saying, "Send her away, for she is crying after us." He answered, "I was sent only to the lost sheep of the house of Israel." But she came and knelt before him, saying, "Lord, help me." And he answered, "It is not fair to take the children's bread and throw it to the dogs." She said, "Yes, Lord, yet even the dogs eat the crumbs that fall from their masters' table." Then Jesus answered her, "O woman, great is your faith! Be it done for you as you desire."[30]

Likewise, the Roman centurion who Jesus also says has great faith does not have the same foundational understanding of Jesus, but he has acquired a new understanding out of the experience of his journey.

As he entered Capernaum, a centurion came forward to him, beseeching him and saying, "Lord, my servant is lying paralyzed at home, in terrible distress." And he said to him, "I will come and heal him." But the centurion answered him, "Lord, I am not worthy

30. Matthew 15:21-28.

to have you come under my roof; but only say the word, and my servant will be healed. For I am a man under authority, with soldiers under me; and I say to one, `Go,' and he goes, and to another, `Come,' and he comes, and to my slave, `Do this,' and he does it." When Jesus heard him, he marveled, and said to those who followed him, "Truly, I say to you, not even in Israel have I found such faith.[31]

In these two instances, faith is not the kind of foundational, common understanding that we call religious faith today. For Jesus, faith was an awareness of a greater presence at work in his life and he recognized a similar faith in the Roman centurion and the Canaanite woman. This kind of faith is not something we inherit or muster and then cling to for security. It is rather a faith that is produced in us through the experience of something greater than ourselves. This is very different from the faith we have in our foundational understanding. The faith we have in our inherited orientation is a faith we grab onto and get a sense of security from if we treat it as sacred. That was the faith of the religious leaders in Jesus day, but the faith of which Jesus speaks is not some understanding to be clung to but an awareness of something greater than ourselves that has the power to change us. The disciple Peter is a great example of this.

And the Lord said, "Simon, Simon, behold, Satan hath desired to have you, that he may sift you as wheat: But I have prayed for thee, that thy faith fail

31.   Matthew 8:5-13, also Luke 7:1-10.

not: and when thou art converted, strengthen thy brethren." And he said unto him, "Lord, I am ready to go with thee, both into prison, and to death." And he said, "I tell thee, Peter, the cock shall not crow this day, before that thou shalt thrice deny that thou knowest me."[32]

This is a strange passage since it appears that Peter's faith did fail that very night since Peter denied knowing Jesus three times. Jesus, however, says that he had prayed in order that Peter's faith would not fail, although Jesus knew that Peter was about to deny knowing him. Obviously, Jesus did not think that Peter's denial marked a failure of his faith. We might think that but it seems Jesus has a very different notion of faith than we do.

Additionally, Jesus says, "When thou art converted, strengthen thy brethren." Surely, Peter must have been converted after having been with Jesus for three years. Peter had been on the Mount of Transfiguration[33] and had walked on water at Jesus' command.[34] Peter had proclaimed that Jesus was "The Messiah, the Son of the living God,"[35] and surely he must have been converted by such experiences. Jesus must be speaking of some deeper conversion.

For Peter that deeper conversion begins on the night that Jesus was arrested. After professing that he was willing to die

32. Luke 22:31-34 KJV.
33. Matthew 17:1-13.
34. Matthew 14:28-32.
35. Matthew 16:16.

with Jesus, Peter denies ever having known him.[36] In that dark night what *we* might consider Peter's faith did fail, but Jesus seems to have known of a deeper faith that was not going to fail. In order to come to that deeper faith, Peter first had to come to see who he really was and who God really was, and that only comes about through a death and resurrection experience. Peter's faith—the faith that he mustered in order to believe in and follow Jesus—had to die in order to receive the deeper faith that comes from God. In order to see who we truly are, the illusion of who we think we are must be destroyed. Peter thinks he knows who he is. He is a devout follower of Jesus for whom he is willing to die if necessary. That night, however, he discovers that despite his best intentions he was not unable to sustain that faith. But as Peter experiences the death of his own faith, and the death of who he thought he was, he is about to see who God truly is.

The revelation of who God truly is comes when Peter encounters the risen Christ. But it is not merely the fact that Peter has witnessed Jesus raised from the dead. What reveals the nature of God is the fact that the risen Christ never mentions Peter's denial but instead gives Peter three chances to say, "I love you."[37] Unlike you or me, who would have something to say to a friend who had failed so miserably in their faithfulness toward us, Jesus never mentions Peter's denial. At that point, Peter must realize that nothing can separate him from Jesus' love, not even his own lack of faith. Prior to that point, Peter

---

36. John 18:17-27.
37. John 21:15-17.

might have known some things about Jesus. He may have even known that Jesus was the Son of God, but it was not until his encounter with the risen Christ that he knew the true nature of the Divine and that nothing could separate him from God's love. This is the ultimate point of faith toward which we are all being drawn, but we only seem to reach it through that dark night of the soul when our own faith is shaken to its core. It is only when we experience God's love after our own faith has failed that we realize that God's love is not a response to our faith.

Of course, the ultimate manifestation of faith through death and resurrection is Jesus himself. In the Gospels, Jesus works miracles, heals the lame, and raises the dead. He does these things faithfully, but the end of his faith journey leads him into rejection, suffering, and what seems to be abandonment by God. The faith journey begins with experiences of God meeting us in our hours of need, but when we eventually come to the point of our greatest need, instead of experiencing God's presence, we experience what appears to be God's absence. Jesus, from the cross, cries, "My God, my God, why have you forsaken me?"[38] Some argue that Jesus is merely quoting Psalm 22—which, no doubt he is—but he is also revealing the sense of abandonment that everyone who sets out on a genuine faith journey ultimately experiences.

Of course, there is a theology that claims that God did abandon Jesus because God cannot be in the presence of sin,

---

38.   Matthew 27:46 and Mark 15:34.

and since Jesus had taken the sin of the world upon himself, God did in fact forsake Jesus. This is what we might believe before the deeper conversion. Our inherited, Christian understanding might have us believing that God loves the righteous and cannot tolerate sin. But Jesus' ministry is all about convincing us that none are righteous and all are sinners in need of God's mercy and forgiveness, which we receive because of who God is and not in exchange for something that we do or believe. The only way we come to that faith is when we are unable to muster any faith of our own and God seems a long way off. Like the story of the footprints in the sand, we can see only one set of footprints, and feel that God is no longer walking with us, while the reality is the footprints are God's and he is carrying us, although we are unaware of His presence in such moments. Jesus models this perfectly when he cries from the cross out of a sense of abandonment.

I once heard someone say that no one was more surprised on Easter Sunday morning than Jesus. To many that may seem blasphemous, and I thought the same thing when I first heard it. Certainly, Jesus knew what was going to happen to him. He had prophesied what was going to happen, so it could not have been a surprise. But it was a surprise in the way that we are all surprised by what seems the absence of God in our hour of need. Jesus had never been distracted from an awareness of his Father's presence the way we so easily are by sin, but when Jesus took the sin of the world upon himself he was distracted from his Father's presence. For the first time in his life he was unable to sense the Divine omnipresence, just as we fail to sense

God's presence because we are constantly distracted from an awareness of it by sin.

This is the great psychological revelation of the cross, but we cannot see it because we have an inherited theological understanding of Jesus as divine and therefore we imagine that his experience is very different from our own. Many dismiss the idea of taking on the Jesus perspective since it is considered blasphemy to think that one can have God's perspective. We do not see things from the perspective of eternity as God does, but what Jesus is offering is not a God's eye view but the ideal perspective of whom we humans should understand God to be and who we should understand ourselves to be in relationship to the Divine. The claim that the God of the universe was his own father, and that we should take on that perspective as well, was blasphemous to the religious leaders of Jesus' day, and is still seen as blasphemous by many today. But even for those who are intent upon making the Jesus perspective their own, it remains something that we never fully grasp until we wake up alive in the tomb.

It is difficult to receive the revelation of the cross—the revelation of death and resurrection—as a revelation about the human condition. We want death and revelation to be about God and not about us. We want Jesus to be pure God, and not man. It is easy to prefer a divine Jesus to a human one because it is easier to worship Jesus than follow him into death and resurrection. But the Gospel story is about the Divine becoming a human being in order to show us how to do this human thing right. The Jesus revelation is that we are God's beloved daughters and sons, and nothing can separate us from our Father's love. This is the ultimate faith of the Jesus perspective, but we ultimately come to that faith only through the kind of death and resurrection experience that Jesus models.

Certainly, Jesus had faith when he was raising the dead and walking on water, but the faith he had on Easter Sunday morning was a different kind of faith. It was the kind of faith that only comes through death and resurrection, and his message is that God wishes us all to come to that ultimate place of faith. We, however, prefer a faith that is based upon our worshipping Jesus through conventional institutions rather than following him into the kind of spiritual journey that he models. Of course, Jesus is worthy of worship and if we don't worship him, we may either deify ourselves or some other less than divine individual. We are to both worship him and follow him, but, if we have trouble doing both, his preference seems to be that we follow him rather than worship him.

In contrast to the many times throughout the Gospels that Jesus says "Follow me,"[39] he never tells us to worship him. Only twice is the phrase "worship me" used in the Gospels. Once is when Satan asks Jesus to worship him.[40] The other is when Jesus quotes the prophet Isaiah.

> Isaiah prophesied rightly about you hypocrites, as it is written, 'This people honors me with their lips, but their hearts are far from me; in vain do they worship me, teaching human precepts as doctrines.'[41]

---

39. Matthew 4:19; 8:22; 9:9; 16:24; 19:21; Mark 2:14; 8:34; 10:21; Luke 5:27; 9:23; 9:59; 18:22; John 1:43; 10:27; 12:26; 13:36; 21:19.
40. Matthew 4:9, also Luke 4:7.
41. Matthew 15:7-9, also Mark 7:6.

Indeed, even when we claim to worship him, it is more often
our own understanding that we worship as sacred. Worshipping
our own understanding is very different from following him into
the mystery of God's mercy. Jesus' teachings are not concerned
with convincing us that he is God incarnate and worthy to be
worshipped, but much more about giving us the Jesus perspective and convincing us that we are God's beloved daughters and
sons. Throughout the four Gospels, Jesus refers to God as either
"our father," "your father," "your heavenly father," or "your
father in heaven" twenty-seven times.[42] This is how Jesus sees
the human condition. It is the truth of his unique perspective.
When he says, "I am the way and the truth"[43] he is offering us
a truth that can serve as the end or second truth of the spiritual
journey to which he calls us.

I often meet Christians who tell me that they have a personal relationship with Jesus Christ, but when I ask them to tell
me about him they quote doctrine and offer theology. They seem
to have no idea of the Jesus perspective or second truth that
Jesus is offering as a conceptual understanding through which
to interpret our spiritual journey. They have no idea that what
is being offered in the Gospel is Jesus' own unique perspective.
He offers us that perspective so we might interpret our experience as he did, and thereby become like him. Those who think
they already have the truth have no idea of the second truth that

----

42. Matthew 5:16; 5:45; 5:48; 6:1; 6:4; 6:6; 6:8; 6:9; 6:15; 6:14;
6:18; 6:26; 6:32; 7:11;10:20; 10:29; 18:14; 18:35; Mark 11:25; Luke
6:36; 10:21; 11:13; 12:30; 12:32; 15:21; John 8:41; 20:17.

43. John 14:6.

Jesus is calling them to follow because they think there is only one truth, which they already have, and anything that does not conform to their understanding of the truth is simply dismissed as untrue.

If we are serious about having a personal relationship with someone we claim to love and wish to emulate—if we really wish to know Jesus—what we are after is not the facts of his life but how he had uniquely come to interpret those facts. What we want to know is the personal understanding or conceptual perspective that guided him in his relationship with God and the world? When Jesus says, "I am ... the truth,"[44] he is speaking of a very different concept of truth than the one we inherit with our foundational understanding. Our inherited concept of truth is not about how one individual conceptualizes the data of their experience but how everyone around us does. Because it is meant to allow us to interpret things the way everyone else does, our inherited, common understanding is thought to be universal and objective, but for those on spiritual journeys there is always a second truth that is the unique personal understanding that is coming out of their encounters with the Divine. This is the truth of which Jesus speaks. It is not a truth about objective reality, but the personal understanding he has come to through his spiritual journey. Unfortunately, when we read the things that Jesus said and did, we generally interpret them either through our own inherited cultural and linguistic tradition, or we go to a Greek lexicon thinking that will get us to some deeper meaning, but it never does. It may bring us closer to the cultural understanding

---

44. John 14:6.

that Jesus inherited but not the authentic understanding of his second truth.

If people say they love Jesus, but what they know of Jesus is no more than objective facts concerning his life, isn't that more a case of celebrity worship rather than a real personal love? We can worship celebrities without knowing them at all, but with those we are really in love with, we seek the truth of who they really are. We spend time in their presence and hopefully come to see things as they understand and interpret them. This is what lies at the base of truly intimate relationships. Of course, time does not permit us to seek to know everyone's second truth, but with those individuals with whom we fall in love, we seek something deeper than the common understanding we share with them and everyone else. With those whom we love, we seek to know the unique way they have come to make sense of their experience. Likewise, we can sense when someone truly wants to know us and get inside our heads in order to see things the way we do. This is the way Jesus wants us to know him. This is the truth to which Jesus calls us and the truth in which we place our faith. It is not a faith in religious doctrine or theology but a faith in the Jesus perspective.

This is a very different concept of faith than the blind acceptance of the religious faith we inherit as part of our foundational understanding. We see these two very different concepts of faith at work throughout the Gospels. There is the faith that the religious leaders of Jesus' day had in the truth of their inherited understanding, and there is a faith in the truth of the Jesus perspective. A faith in the truth of the Jesus perspective is not a faith that we have to defend because it is not a faith that we possess. The truth of the Jesus perspective is always more radical than we would like to imagine, and it is always out in front beckoning us to follow as we fall more deeply in love with him and wish to know him more intimately.

We see these two faiths at work in the Gospels and they are what create the division between those who follow Jesus and those who oppose him. These two groups of people are both people of faith, but while the one group has faith in their foundational understanding, the other group has a faith in a new understanding that is coming out of their experience of following Jesus. This is still the great divide among people of faith. Christians are divided today, not over superficial matters like being Protestants or Catholics, but rather over whether they put their faith in inherited Christian truths or set out on a journey in pursuit of the authentic and personal second truth that is the Jesus perspective.

The closer we come to the Jesus perspective, however, the more we should realize how far we are from it. The mind of Christ was constantly aware of his Father's presence. Our minds, however, are constantly distracted from an awareness of that divine presence. I believe this is the central theme that underlies what Jesus is trying to tell us in The Sermon on the Mount; that is, that our real sin is not found in our behavior but in the fact that we are constantly distracted from the Father's presence in a way that Jesus never was. Long before we commit adultery or murder we are distracted from an awareness of God's presence by our lust or anger. Likewise, Jesus warns us of things like worry, earthly treasure, and judgment.[45] These are the things that keep us from an awareness of God's presence and the fullness of life that comes with that awareness. Not only does Jesus have a very different concept of sin, but he also tells us to love our enemies.[46] By definition, however, our enemies are people that we do not love. Apparently, our idea of love and his are very different. Add to this the fact that nearly everyone dislikes the parable where the workers who only work the last hour get the same as those who have labored all day.[47] All of this testifies to how radically different the mind of Christ is from the minds that have been given us by our culture, history, and language communities but perhaps the most radical concept Jesus presents is found in the story of the Prodigal.[48] There the prodigal son does it wrong but that turns out to be honored, and the older son does it right and that turns out to produce a feeling of dishonor. If anyone reads the Gospels and considers the things that Jesus says about things like faith, sin, love, forgiveness, and truth it should be obvious that he has very different concepts of such things than the concepts we received as part of our inherited understanding.

Jesus turns the world upside down, but most of us refuse to go there with him and only take in those aspects of Jesus' teachings that fit with our inherited understanding. His more radical concepts are generally ignored even by those who consider

---

45. Matthew 5:1-7:17.
46. Matthew 5:44; Luke 6:27
47. Matthew 20:1-16.
48. Luke 15:11-32.

themselves his devout followers. So long as we consider our inherited cultural concepts to be sacred, we read the Gospel through them, rather than allowing Jesus' teachings to do violence to that inherited understanding in order that we might begin to take on the heart of Jesus.

The great philosophers did not tell us about the world, but about how they had uniquely come to conceptualize the world and therein make sense of their experience. The same is true of Jesus. Just as the intellectual journey, which Socrates called philosophy, is the pursuit of a second truth, the spiritual journey to which Jesus calls us is equally the pursuit of a second truth. Furthermore, this second truth is also what we seek when we want to know any person on a deep, personal level. Authentic individuals always have a second truth, and when we wish to know such individuals this is the truth we are after. If we claim to really know another person it is not that we know some facts about their life, but rather that we know something of the unique conceptual understanding through which they make sense of that life.

CHAPTER FOUR

The Second Truth of the Other

AS WE BEGAN to see in the last chapter, this second truth is not only the better conceptual understanding we seek for ourselves, but also what we really wish to know in our more intimate relationships with others. The most interesting conversations I have are with people who also are in pursuit of this second truth and are willing to talk about it. The most interesting books I have ever read are those in which the authors share their unique and authentic way of interpreting their experience. These are the authentic conversations and authentic people who confirm the hope within us that there is a greater truth than what we have inherited as our initial orientation to the world.

So, it is not just *our* second truth that we are interested in but also the second truth of others. What we find interesting about Copernicus, Newton, Einstein, and Heidegger, and what we should find most interesting about Jesus, is the unique way they come to interpret their experience. They are not telling us about the world but the unique way they have come to conceptualize the world. It is their philosophy or the second truth that they are crafting out of their unique experience. They are giving us a glimpse into their own understanding, which, in the case of Copernicus, Newton, or Einstein, we, in time, imagine is not their understanding at all but rather the way things actually are. The reason this happens is that once a particular perspective is shared and becomes popular, it is passed on to subsequent generations as the foundational truth of their initial understanding. At this stage it is no longer recognized as the perspective of an individual but as an objective and certain truth. This is how civilization advances.

Since we inherit our initial orientation to the world at an early age from others who hold positions of authority, we never question this understanding, nor should we until we gain a certain maturity. Furthermore, even when we do begin to question our initial orientation and set out in search of a better perspectival understanding, we still retain our initial orientation as the basis for much of our social interaction. As we have discussed, our social interactions with others is usually on the basis of our initial understanding rather than the second truth we are pursuing.

When, however, we wish to establish a more intimate communion with another person, what we often want to know is how that individual has come to uniquely conceptualize and interpret their experience. Deep, intimate conversations are generally philosophical conversations insofar as what we want to know concerns how that individual has come to uniquely conceptualize their experience. When we read the great philosophers, we might naively think that they are talking about some external reality, but in fact they are always talking about how they uniquely conceptualize that reality. They are giving us a glimpse into their own heads and how they have come to conceptualize and interpret the data of their experience. I remember a fellow student telling me that she had read so much Sartre that she felt that she had had an affair with him.

We want to imagine that truth is something greater than our own perspective, and it is in almost every way. Our initial orientation is greater than our own perspective because it is shared by a great many people, and the second truth that we are in search of is always greater than our present understanding, but the second truth of another person is also always beyond us. If we think it is not and that they conceptualize things exactly as we do, our relationship will never go to that deeper, more intimate level. When we really wish to know another human being what we are really after is the unique way that they are coming to understand and interpret their experience. That is what makes each individual life authentic. Some of these authentic individuals become the Newtons and Einsteins of history, but our loved ones often have their own second truth if we take time to search for it.

Sadly, we all too often suppose that there is only one truth and when we encounter others, we imagine that the understanding through which they interpret the world must be the same as ours. When we discover that it is not, we dismiss them as stupid or wrong-headed for not having the true perspective that we have. Of course, if we are aware of a second truth, and open ourselves to perspectives not our own, deeper and more intimate communion with others becomes possible. This encounter with the second truth of another is a large piece of what intimacy is really all about. Nel Noddings describes it beautifully:

> I am having lunch with a group of colleagues. Among them is one for whom I have never had much regard

and for whom I have little professional respect. I do not care for him. Somewhere in the light banter of lunch talk, he begins to talk about an experience in the wartime navy and the feelings he had under a particular treatment. He talks about how his feelings impelled him to become a teacher. His expressions are unusually lucid, defenseless. I am touched—not only by sentiment—but by something else. It is as though his eyes and mine have combined to look at the scene he describes. I know I would have behaved differently in the situation, but this is in itself a matter of indifference. I feel what he says he felt. I have been invaded by this other. Quite simply, I shall never again be completely without regard for him.[49]

Likewise, when a person dies and we hear another say, "I wish I had got to know her better" the reference is not to knowing more facts about the person's life. It is not that there is a lack of an objective truth about the person. That is not what is regretted. The regret is never having come to know how that person uniquely understood and interpreted his or her experience. This is the regret we hear from so many: that they never got to know a certain person who was very dear but unknown to them.

I've experienced that regret in regard to my father, whom I never knew. Well, I did know him, but he died when I was 18 and I never got to have those deeper conversations that would have brought me to really know the truth of who he was and how he had tried to make sense of his experience. Certainly, I

---

49. Noddings. *Caring.* 30.

knew some facts about his life, but I didn't know the mystery behind those facts, the mystery that caused him to interpret and react to circumstances the way he did. I knew he was born in Ireland and came to America in his early twenties. I even knew that he had only gone through the third grade. That in itself was something of a mystery since he had two sons, both of whom got Ph.Ds. The odds against an Irish immigrant with a third grade education having two sons (and one of them a crow) both getting Ph.Ds. have to be astronomical.

Our father had a gruff exterior, but he could cry at the drop of a hat. I've often wondered whether it was a genetic thing or if it was Ireland that did that to him. He immigrated to America in the 1920s and had been here twenty-five years when I was born, but when he thought of Ireland, he always came apart. In the 1950s, Arthur Godfrey had a variety show on television and he always had a St. Patrick's Day special with Carmel Quinn and other Irish singers and dancers. My poor father would look forward to it for weeks, but when the show would finally air, he would only last about five minutes before he would burst out crying and run into the bathroom. He was that way at funerals, too. I remember, as a kid, being embarrassed at funerals, because out of nowhere he would wail. I know it's OK for men to cry but this was wailing. I think I feared that I might have that same gene, or maybe it was some weird Irish thing that I might have inherited.

Most men suppress and never make a show of sadness. Of course, they can cry and show emotion over a nostalgic sports moment, but they find it enormously difficult to cry or even talk about genuine sadness. Ask your father what was the saddest day of his life, and he'll find some way to refuse to talk about it. Most men won't go there. Well, that was not my father. He was very expressive concerning sadness and he expressed it with wailing.

I remember my mother telling me a story long after he had died about their wedding reception. They were married seven years after he had been in this country, and at the wedding reception my mother met a couple from whom my father rented a room the first five years he was in this country. They told my mother that they listened to him cry himself to sleep every night for those first five years. I never understood that nor did I want to, for fear of having that Irish thing in me, but because I never understood that, I never really knew my father on that deeper intimate level. I'm sure if he were alive today, that is what I would want to know—what was behind that crying? What was it about the way he had come to understand and interpret the world that made him respond to his experience in that way?

About ten years after my father died, I did get a little glimpse into the mystery of what must have been his understanding and the truth of his life. I read Leon Uris' *Trinity*. It was about the Irish quest for home rule, but the part of the book that particularly spoke to me was the idea of being "up for immigration." The Irish economy could not support any increase in population; the eldest male child would inherit the family property and the other siblings were "up for immigration." I tell my students, imagine going home today and your parents sit you down at the kitchen table. "Nora, you know you're up for immigration, and we'll be taking you to the boat on Saturday." What is the understanding that you have to form to bear and make sense of that reality? That's what I would have wanted to know about my father—how did he understand and make sense of that. Years later, I got a little more insight.

I received a phone call one day from a woman with a heavy Irish brogue. She said she had seen my name in the phone book and wanted to know if we were related. It turned out she was my first cousin, and here in New York on business. I invited her for dinner, and over conversation I discovered that she grew up in the same house as my father. Not knowing much about Ireland except what I had learned from Uris' *Trinity*, and being woefully ignorant of the Irish side of my family, I mentioned to her that her father was the oldest of the nine siblings, since he inherited the family property. She told me I was mistaken, and that my father was the oldest, but he left and went to America in order that her father wouldn't have to immigrate.

Ten years after I met that cousin in the States, I made a trip to Ireland with my brother, and visited her and her ninety-year-old mother. They still lived in the same house—the house my father grew up in—and when this aunt of mine whom I had just met for the first time, began in her Irish brogue to tell me about my father and grandfather, I lost it, and had to run to the bathroom, as I remember my father so often doing on St. Patrick's Day. After I had cleaned myself up and pulled myself together, I returned, but when she started talking again, I lost it for a second time. Later, I told my brother, "Go over and sit by her" to which he replied, "I ain't going over there."

One thing I vividly remember about that conversation I had with my aunt was her telling me about my grandfather, whom, of course, I had never met. She referred to him affectionately as "Sir", as if that was his first name. As she spoke, I couldn't help thinking: I wish he had written something—something that could reveal a little of the mystery that he was, that we all are—something of the truth of his understanding. What I wanted was some deeper connection with this grandfather who had such an important influence upon my life, but I had little way of knowing him apart from this old woman's stories.

I don't know what that uncontrollable emotion was all about, and it certainly rekindled my fear that I had inherited my father's crying gene, but it also confirmed my belief that the truth of this human thing is much more mysterious than we have been led to believe. If we wish to know the truth of another human being or even the truth of ourselves, it is a very different kind of truth that we are after. When we made the paradigm of the natural sciences the model for all knowledge, we truncated our notion of truth and therein made our quest for intimacy something other than a quest for truth—the truth of the other.

Aristotle said that human beings are involved in a three-fold existence. We are involved in doing, making, and knowing. In doing, we want to do what is good, in making, we want to make what is beautiful, and in knowing we want to know what is true. Unfortunately, our modern notion of truth equated truth with facticity rather than the understanding through which the facts are interpreted. Thankfully, we are finally at a point in our human history where we are aware of the perspectival nature of all facts and thus we have to consider the truth of the understanding that produces our interpretation of the facts: either the truth of our foundational understanding, or the second, philosophical truth that begins to emerge when we set out in search of better ways to conceptualize and interpret our experience.

A major difference between these two truths is that the second truth should never be possessed in the way that we possess the truth of our initial understanding. As we saw with Socrates, the second truth is always a provisional truth that marks the stages of a dialogue and is never the last word. That is also the case when we are pursuing the second truth of another person. There is always more that they have to say, and the understanding that is unique to them—their second truth—always requires further articulation.

Unlike Copernicus or Newton, most of us have never tried to articulate our second truth. Of course, some simply do not have much in the way of a second truth and never really enter into a philosophical stage but retain their foundational understanding all of their lives. Others have had the circumstances of their lives change their conceptual perspective but have no one with whom to articulate their unique second truth. Many people enter therapy because they lack an intimate other with whom they can authenticate themselves by articulating how their experience has uniquely shaped the conceptual understanding through which they interpret the world.

Sadly, the modern minds we inherited as our foundational understanding gave us the notion that there was but one truth that was universal and objective, and had nothing to do with the unique way we perceive the world. That, however, was to deny the truth of the individual and we have seen the inhumane effects of that throughout the 20th century. The modern idea of a single, objective, and universal truth provided the basis for the rise of fascist and totalitarian regimes in the 20th century, and equally the rise of an existential response to the terror that comes from not recognizing the truth of the individual.

Certainly, we can speak of truth in terms of facts interpreted by an understanding that is common to many people within the same culture and language community, but to believe that is the only way to think about truth is naïve with what we now know about the interpretive nature of the human condition. Such a limited notion of truth has made for a very impersonal world where there are no personal truths, only the collective lockstep truth to which we were all taught to march. We are constantly pressured to conform to the truth of the understanding that is set before us by our history, culture, and language community, but when we really love others and want to know them on that more intimate level, one of the things that we want to know about them is how they have come to uniquely conceptualize and interpret their experience.

As we have said, seeking to know the truth of another individual is very different from what we have been taught concerning truth and how it should be sought. We were told that all knowing was to be like scientific knowing—objective and factual, but knowing a person is very different. It is about connecting on a deeper level. When others with whom we are intimate say, "You don't understand," what they are usually saying is that we are not seeing things from their perspective; we are not in their head, and if we really wanted to know them, we would make every effort to adopt their perspective and see what they are talking about from their unique understanding. Human intimacy and closeness happens when we capture a glimpse of someone else's conceptual perspective.

I often tell my students that philosophy will help them in their intimate relationships later in life. When we study Plato, Berkeley, Hume, or Heidegger what we are doing is trying to get inside their heads and see as they saw. If we can learn to do that, then when our spouse or child tells us that we don't understand, we know what they are talking about because we didn't understand Plato when we first encountered him, but if we made the effort to know these philosophers, we were developing the ability to know as another person knows. When I hear people pooh-pooh philosophy it can often mean that they do not have much in the way of intimate relationships since they are very content with their own perspective and not interested in perspectives that are not their own. If you have loved ones, you may wish that they could see as you see, but they can't get out of their own heads and take on your perspective.

I have met many people who claim to have a personal relationship with Jesus, but they don't seem to really want to know the unique conceptual perspective through which he interpreted his experience, and isn't that what it means to really know the truth of another person? If someone desires to know others on a personal level, they are not after objective facts but the personal understanding through which they interpret their circumstances.

This is the deep spiritual connection we are all looking for with those we love most. Unfortunately, several factors make it difficult to know how other people have come to uniquely conceptualize their experience. To begin with, such knowledge has to be revelatory. They have to want to reveal their understanding to us, because unlike the data of our everyday experience, the second truth of others is hidden and has to be revealed by them. This is an enormous barrier, since even if the persons are willing, which they often are not for multiple reasons, it is not easy to find words that will express their unique understanding. Perhaps great writers have that ability, but it is difficult at best for most of us. Secondly, we have to be willing to receive the revelation, and there are numerous obstacles to this as well. A major obstacle is that we have been taught that there is only one truth and it is universal and objective; when someone has a unique understanding we simply want that person to stop thinking that way and return to the understanding of the herd. Most people who have never progressed beyond the first truth have no interest in the second truth of another because they do not see it as truth at all but rather as some ailment or abnormality. Indeed, in some cases one's second truth may be classified as a disorder and therapy may be needed to restore an individual to a healthier perspective, but along with such cases there are also those whose second truth provides a better perspective through which to interpret our experience. Few of us have second truths that eventually become the foundational truths of future generations, but most people do begin to form second truths in at least some area in order to accommodate the uniqueness of their own experience. Furthermore, that second truth should be of interest to those with whom we are most intimate. When your spouse says,

"You don't understand," what they usually mean is that you are not interpreting a situation from their perspectival understanding. It takes effort and practice to get out of one's own head and see the world through the unique understanding of another person. There is something of a second truth in most of us, but only those who really wish to know us on a deeper and more intimate level take the time to know that unique understanding. Of course, long before we can go to that depth with another person, we have to acknowledge that there is a second truth or personal way that other individuals have come to interpret their experience.

In teaching philosophy to first-time students, I find that many have no idea of a second truth and still treat their foundational understanding as the only truth. I tell them that unless they become aware of a second truth and learn how to access it in others they will never go to much depth in their personal relationships. Since they assume that there is nothing beyond the truth of their initial orientation, they will judge the perspective of others right or wrong, true or false, by whether it conforms or fails to conform to their own foundational understanding. Furthermore, even if they do come to realize that there are other perspectives than their own, they will have no knowledge of how to access the truth of that other perspective.

Thus, we study philosophy for essentially two reasons. First, to teach us how to pursue and access an ever better conceptual understanding for ourselves, and therein provide a fuller and more fruitful interpretation of the experience that is an authentic life. And second, in order to learn how to access perspectives that are different from our own. When we study Plato, Aristotle, Augustine, Descartes, Locke, or Heidegger, we are not learning primarily about the world, but about how certain individuals had come to uniquely conceptualize the world. By doing so we not only become aware of the existence of a second truth but we begin to develop the ability to access the second truth of others. This has a very practical application. When a wife tells her husband that he doesn't understand, the husband, who has become aware of perspectives not his own and developed something of an ability to explore such alternative perspectives, can achieve an intimacy with his wife that is not accessible to those who imagine that there is only one true perspective: their own. For those who cannot imagine a perspective other than their own, critical thinking means that they reject all ideas that do not conform to their perspectival understanding. Their spouses, children, and best friends must say things their way or have what they are saying rejected as simply wrong or false. They have *the* truth, which they see as certain and sacred, and consequently, they lack the capacity to get outside their own heads and encounter another from the perspective of that other person. They may debate their perspective with others but they will never enter into a dialogue in an attempt to encounter and embrace the perspective of another. That can only be done when we hold our own perspective loosely and see it as a provisional truth that changes throughout our journey. Only then can we enter into the kind of dialogue that can bring us to truly know another person.

CHAPTER FIVE

Our Dialogic Pursuit of the Second Truth

A DIALOGUE IS THE MEANS by which we attempt to know the second truth of another. That is very different from the way we came to know our first truth. The first truth was simply given and we acquired it uncritically. Once acquired, that truth is defended with debates. Debates are between people who wish to show how superior their own perspective is to contrary views. One's second truth is not debatable, for there is nothing to defend since we pursue rather than possess the second truth.

I recently saw a website that said, "A debate resolves an issue, but a dialogue just muddies the water." Indeed, a dialogue is a messy matter, but the only thing a debate resolves is that one person is a better debater than the other. Real learning, beyond our initial orientation, is a messy matter since it requires the admission that we do not know the way we would like to know. Debates have nothing to do with learning but are rather a defense of what we have already learned. A dialogue, on the other hand, is the pursuit of a truth we have yet to know.

The classic form of a dialogue consists of a thesis, an antithesis, and a synthesis. In the Platonic dialogues, Socrates' interlocutors usually provide the thesis; they set forth what they hold to be true. Socrates then provides the antithesis or the problem with what the interlocutor believes to be true. The antithesis is never critical of some factual state of affairs but about how the interlocutor conceives of something. It is about one's conceptual understanding and why that conceptual understanding is wrong or needs further articulation. The interlocutor then offers a synthesis in an attempt to accommodate Socrates' criticism. That synthesis then represents a new thesis that Socrates responds to with yet another antithesis. With bad interlocutors, the dialogue usually ends with the interlocutors getting frustrated after several syntheses continue to be met with yet more antitheses. They want things finished and resolved, and give up in frustration when Socrates continues to show their understanding lacking. By contrast, Socrates is never frustrated, because he understands that the second truth is always out of reach but nevertheless always worth pursuing.

I had once thought that Platonic dialogues contained both intelligent and unintelligent interlocutors. I supposed that intelligence was the factor that allowed some interlocutors to go deeper into a dialogue with Socrates than others, but I no longer believe that to be the case. It is not intelligence that determines how far the dialogue goes but rather that some interlocutors are still under the sway of their foundational truths, while others have set out on a journey to find a second truth. In other words, some of the interlocutors are ready for the journey and some are not.

In order for interlocutors to be ready for a Platonic dialogue with Socrates, they must have already entered into an internal dialogue within themselves. In other words, antitheses must already have arisen within them in opposition to their initial, inherited understanding. If they have already faced this conflict within themselves and sought some synthesis or better understanding, they are ready for Socrates and turn out to be good interlocutors. If, however, they are still under the sway of their foundational understanding and see no reason to question it, they simply want to debate with Socrates and defend their own understanding.

Socrates himself represents the kind of mind that is an internal dialogue. Plato even tells us that Socrates has a daemon or spirit that speaks to him. This daemon never tells him what to do or think but only corrects him when there is something wrong with his understanding. This daemon is mentioned in several of Plato's dialogues and represents the antithesis within Socrates' internal dialogue. Just as his daemon provides the antithesis when his understanding needs correction, Socrates provides the antithesis for his interlocutors whose understanding requires rectifying. Notice in both cases neither the daemon nor Socrates provides a synthesis. They merely reveal the necessity for a better understanding. Likewise, when that better understanding is reached in the form of a synthesis, even that understanding carries with it another antithesis which points to a still better understanding.

Unfortunately, most of the people of Athens were not interested in heeding Socrates the way he heeded his *daemon*. They were content with their inherited understanding and had no interest in suspending it in order to enter into the liminal space that all true dialogues require. Most of us are that way. We don't mind a debate where both parties firmly hold onto their own understanding, but a dialogue requires that we heed each antithesis and abandon our previous thesis in the hope of finding a better one. The purpose of a debate is to prove that our perspective is superior and does not need improvement, but a dialogue takes serious the other position (antithesis) and incorporates it into the new understanding toward which we are moving. We are not ready for a dialogue until we reach a place where the security that our foundational truth provides is no longer indispensable and we can move beyond it in search of a mysterious second truth.

Our human psyche requires that we begin with a belief in the absolute truth of our foundational orientation. As long as we are still there the most we can ever do is to debate those whose perspective is different from our own. Some, however, reach an age where their initial understanding is no longer as sacred as it had been and they are able to move beyond it and enter into genuine dialogue with others whose perspectival understanding is very different than their own. More than the fact that we have different views on politics or religion, what really separates us as people is that at the heart of the human condition there are two very different truths, and people pledge allegiance either to one or the other. The one group sees their foundational truth as absolute and sacred, while others see their foundational truth as the safe harbor from which they set out on a journey in pursuit of an illusive second truth. Those who wish to defend their foundational truth are the debaters who seek to refute all antitheses, while the other group welcomes a dialogue and the antitheses that encourage them to seek a greater understanding.

The defenders of the foundational truth are usually the dominant group. They have an advantage in that everyone in their society starts out from their truth. Additionally, they are almost always the more socially powerful group who wish to maintain their position of privilege that is based upon their foundational understanding remaining intact. A second truth is always dangerous to those in power since it threatens the truth upon which their power rests. In the past, those who pursued a second truth were often eliminated or tortured into returning to the foundational understanding. Those who pursue a second truth are better off today, but they still have little to support them in their pursuit except the mystical faith to believe that a better understanding exists.

A dialogue in pursuit of a better understanding is always mysterious, since it requires that we abandon the understanding with which we are familiar in order to get to a better understanding. But why would we think that there is a better way to interpret our experience, especially after having read the Platonic dialogues where Socrates continues to pursue a truth that is always out of reach? It is fine for him to show us that there is something wrong with the interlocutors' understanding but seldom does he have anything better to offer than the liminal space of an ongoing dialogue and a mystical faith in a second truth.

The modern faith of most religious people is about having an unshakeable belief in their foundational understanding, but the faith that is needed in order to pursue a second truth requires a mystical faith that a better understanding exists and is worth pursuing even if never realized. These are the two different faiths that exist today. The difference between Protestants and Catholics or Jews and Muslims is superficial in comparison to the difference between people who put their faith in their inherited, foundational understanding and those whose faith is in this mysterious second truth that they pursue rather than possess. Those who put their faith in their foundational truth are not interested in an intellectual or spiritual dialogue after a better understanding. They want only to defend the truth which they already possess. They like the illusion that winning a debate confirms the truth of their understanding. In fact, however, all it really means is that they lack the courage to venture out in pursuit of a truth that is greater than their own understanding. They may say that they have faith, but it is a faith in their own understanding, while real faith is always in something greater than our understanding. That is the kind of faith that fuels an intellectual or spiritual journey.

These two different notions of truth are encountered with two very different forms of intelligence and spirituality. If we identify with the first truth of our initial orientation then our educational and religious institutions are more about providing us with a safe harbor where we can feel secure, rather than setting us out on a journey. Such institutions try to convince us that intelligent people are those who quickly and accurately record the information given them and the spiritual people are those who are unwavering in their religious beliefs. Sadly, those are the very people who killed both Socrates and Jesus. Both were killed by people defending truth, that is, the foundational understanding they held to be sacred. Throughout our history, much more violence has been done in defense of truth than out of anger. Wars are fought not because soldiers from one side are angry at soldiers from the other camp but because each side is defending a truth that they see as sacred. Our war dead were great patriots but not the war dead of our enemies. They were mere fanatics because they were not fighting for *truth*. Of course, what we mean by truth is the foundational orientation of our culture and language community. If we are to survive as a species, we must get beyond this idea that our foundational truths are sacred. It is fine and even necessary for children to believe that, but with age we should begin to see the mythic nature of that inherited truth and set out in search of a greater understanding. Sadly, even when we do enter into such a journey, our tendency is to think that any new insight we come to is *the* truth: the ultimate understanding, which simply replaces our foundational orientation and resupplies us with a sense of certainty. Few of us are willing to live in the liminal space of a dialogue and be those who Socrates says are the "better and braver"[50] human beings who are open to learning and live on the threshold of an ever new understanding.

Debates may be about what we hold to be true, but dialogues are always based upon the idea that there is a better way to understand things. That better understanding cannot be pursued unless we allow those antitheses that come into our lives to do violence to what we think we know. Debates are for the quick

---

50. Plato. *Meno*. 86b4-c1.

and clever who not only believe that they know the truth, but can defend it vigorously. Dialogues, on the other hand, are for those humbler souls who can easily yield their position, since they don't take much pride in what they think they know. While debates are all about what we know, dialogues are about faith in the hope that there is a better way to understand what we are talking about. In a dialogue we are constantly asking questions; in a debate we are merely giving answers. What a shame that so many of our world religions center on debates over what they proclaim rather than journeys into a better way to understand and interpret our experience with the divine.

As we have seen, two great examples of lives lived in such liminality are those of Socrates and Jesus. Contrary to what many might believe, neither Socrates nor Jesus put a high premium on what they knew. Both were much more concerned with the pursuit of truth rather than the ego gratification that comes from believing that they had attained it. The Platonic dialogues seldom come to conclusions, not simply because of bad interlocutors, but because what Socrates is pursuing is always out of reach; there is always a more ideal perspective or a better way to conceptualize things.

In a similar way, Jesus leads us into a journey but does not give us the kind of truth we want. He says that he is the truth.[51] A truth that is a person is very different from the concept of a foundational truth. It is the truth of his personal understanding, which is constantly open to what he hears from his Father, just as Socrates is constantly open to his *daemon*. Both Socrates

51. John 14:6.

and Jesus are grounded in a mystical, internal dialogue rather than some foundational knowledge that they hold as sacred. It is never a truth that they possess but one that they are open to. That is the nature of the second truth that so many people refuse to follow since it is never something we can possess but rather something that possesses us.

Jesus is not trying to give his disciples a new foundational truth to replace what they inherited. He, like Socrates, honors his foundational truth, and he is attempting to teach his disciples how to live in the same liminal dialogue with God that he does. Like Socrates, he refuses to give answers and satisfy his followers' desire for a truth that they could possess in order to feel secure in their knowledge. In fact, of the 183 questions asked of Jesus throughout the Gospels, he answers only a handful.[52] Jesus' normal response is to ask a question in return, to answer a question other than the one asked, or to simply remain silent. He is not interested in giving us answers so we might feel secure in what we know. Instead, like Socrates, his teachings focus mostly on explaining that our understanding is wrong. He is turning our world upside down, telling us, "the last will be first, and the first

52. Jesus does answer the following questions when asked: Lord, teach us to pray. (Luke 11:1); What is the greatest commandment? (Matthew 22:37); How many times are we to forgive? (Matthew18:21–22). There may also be an answer to a question by the rich young ruler (Matthew 19:16–22). The other two are questionable as to whether they are actually answers. Jesus is asked: "Are you the son of God?" And he answers, "You say that I am" (Luke 22:69–70); Or, "Are you the king of the Jews?" Jesus again says, "You say so" (Matthew 27:11; Mark 15:2).

will be last,"[53] and those who labor all day get the same pay as those who labor only one hour.[54] He tells us that there is more rejoicing in Heaven over one repentant sinner than ninety-nine righteous persons who have no need to repent.[55] And as we saw in an earlier chapter, he tells us a story of two sons: one who does it wrong and that turns out to be good, while the other son does it right and that turns out to be bad.[56] Even more radically he says, "Whoever comes to me and does not hate father and mother, wife and children, brothers and sisters, yes, and even life itself, cannot be my disciple."[57] If we ever took Jesus seriously, we would realize that he is certainly doing violence to our understanding. The Sermon on the Mount is probably the most radical thing ever written. He condemns as sinful what we find innocuous or at least something other than sin. He declares that anger is equivalent to murder,[58] and lust is the same as adultery.[59] He tells us we are not to worry,[60] judge,[61] or love earthly goods,[62] but we are to love our enemies,[63] and "If you do not forgive others, neither will your Father forgive your trespasses."[64]

---

53. Matthew 20:16.
54. Matthew 20:1-15.
55. Luke 15:7.
56. Luke 15:11-32.
57. Luke 14:26.
58. Matthew 5:21-22.
59. Matthew 5:27-28.
60. Matthew 6:25.
61. Matthew 7:1-2.
62. Matthew 6:19-21.
63. Matthew 5:43-48.
64. Matthew 6:15.

He is doing violence to our foundational understanding and attempting to draw us into a journey in pursuit of his greater perspective. We, however, refuse to let that happen and instead either ignore what he says or choose to interpret it in ways that conform to our inherited understanding. We do not allow ourselves to be drawn into a journey in pursuit of Jesus' second truth, which is the perspectival understanding through which Jesus is interpreting his experience.

It is extraordinary that people who claim to believe that Jesus is God incarnate constantly interpret his words in ways that conform to our conventional concepts rath er than allow his words to do violence to our own conceptual understanding and therein draw us ever closer to his divine perspective. We naively imagine that he has the same foundational understanding that we have, instead of trying to learn of his unique perspective. Christians often make following Jesus into believing in doctrines that are held to be objective truths, but that is the foundational truth that eventually has to be abandoned if one is really to follow Jesus and attempt to take on his perspective and see as he saw. For those who seriously follow Jesus, their lives are not founded upon some doctrinal certainty but rather upon the pursuit of the divine perspective that Jesus offers.

In order to pursue such a perspective, however, people have to loosen their hold on their foundational orientation. Many people find this difficult since it means giving up the security that comes from believing that their initial understanding is certain. The idea of a second truth or better perspective always threatens people with great security needs. Notice how angry those opponents of Jesus and Socrates get and how they eventually resort to violence in order to preserve the certainty of their understanding. The Jesus story attests to how fearful the religious leaders in Jesus' day were, just as the Socrates story is a great example of the fears of the Athenians. Likewise, consider the violence in the American south during the 1960s over the civil rights movement. We often dismiss that as hatred but it was more deeply a fear within some individuals of losing their foundational understanding, which they saw as a sacred truth. We see a similar anger and violent reaction among many religious fundamentalists who think they are using violence in defense of truth whereas in fact they are fiercely defending their own egos and the understanding upon which those egos rest. They respond violently because they fear losing their hold on the only truth they know, but that is because they have little experience with a second truth that could provide a better perspective.

Of course, there is good reason to want to unquestioningly preserve our foundational truth. Holding it as absolutely certain gives us a way to quickly and precisely assess whether data is true by its conformity to our understanding. That is a benefit in many situations, since most of our actions require an immediate and thoughtless response, but when that becomes the exclusive way we make judgments it creates a very limited human experience. What Jesus and Socrates offer is very different; they are not offering a new foundation to replace the old, but a very different kind of understanding that is never more than provisional and always points toward some yet greater truth. That is the nature of the liminal reality of a dialogue. It is not easy to live in that liminal space. We much prefer a solid understanding from which to make our judgments and feel secure in them, but if those judgments are always based on whether or not something conforms to our conceptual understanding, we limit our human experience to what is in our own head. Sometimes we need to allow the data of our experience to change what is in our head. A large part of wisdom lies in knowing when to utilize our foundational understanding as the basis for our judgments and when to allow the data of our experience to change that understanding.

There is a Leo Strauss quote that I have framed and hung on the wall of my office. It says that human beings, "...are constantly attracted and deluded by two opposite charms: the charm of competence which is engendered by mathematics and everything akin to mathematics, and the charm of humble awe, which is engendered by meditation on the human soul and its experiences. Philosophy is characterized by a gentle, if firm, refusal to succumb to either charm."[65] The one charm offers certainty and the sense of security that comes from that, while the other opens us to experiences that lie beyond our understanding. A mature and healthy mind never allows one of these charms to totally possess them. We all begin on the side of conventional certainty and at a certain point if we are to grow intellectually and spiritually we need to see that our unique experience is more than our inherited understanding can account for and we need to change that understanding in order to accommodate the data of our experience.

---

65. Quoted in Seth Benardete's *The Being of the Beautiful*, xvii.

Our natural prejudice is to defend and preserve our own conceptual understanding, but if that is the limit of our rationality we have a very truncated notion of reason along with a truncated notion of truth. Indeed, an essential aspect of reason in its highest form is the ability to be impartial; when people lack impartiality we see that as less than rational. The late Louis Pojman had a great example of this in one of his books. Imagine that Notre Dame is playing SMU in football. Obviously, the Notre Dame Coach is not impartial in interpreting what is happening on the field. Neither is the SMU Coach. The referee, on the other hand, is the voice of reason and is supposed to see things impartially. But what if right before the game the referee finds out that his wife has bet their life savings on Notre Dame? Can he still be impartial? Pojman gives an interesting answer. He says, he would have to be a very good referee. All human beings find themselves in the position of that referee. We all have vested interests and want to use reason to defend those interests, but the higher level of reason requires that we suspend our self-interest and consider the data impartially. This is the higher, philosophical stage of human consciousness. Many may say that is impossible and self-interest will always win out, but it depends upon what one's self-interest is. Certainly, if one's self interest is money it will be very hard for that referee to be impartial, but if his interest is to be the best possible referee, then impartiality is not so far-fetched. Likewise, if we are committed to an intellectual or spiritual journey instead of preserving the truth of our conceptual understanding, then impartiality and the higher levels of reason and spirituality become a possibility.

Philosophy and theology make claims to being rational, but they often lack the impartiality so essential to rationality. They are often mere apologetics in defense of their own understanding and little different from the form of rationality exercised by the Notre Dame or SMU coaches. That is very different from what Socrates and Jesus offer and, likewise, why we have to turn to Aristotle for philosophy and Paul for theology. You can't create a philosophical system out of what Socrates says, and you can't make a theological system out of what Jesus says. Both call us to follow a truth that is greater than our own understanding, a truth—as we have repeatedly said—we will never possess but a truth that will possess us and continually draw us to itself.

Both Socrates and Jesus call us to a journey and all they offer is the kind of mind one needs to make such a journey. This is the new wine of which Jesus speaks. He tells us that it cannot be put in an old wineskin but requires a new wineskin.[66] Indeed, this new mind is not a better foundational understanding to replace our initial orientation, but the kind of mind we need to go on a journey into a mystical truth that is always beyond us. Both Socrates and Jesus remind us that there is much more to know than our understanding will allow and therefore we need to constantly change our understanding in order to take in more of what lies before us. This is the ultimate truth of our human condition, and it stands in dire contrast to the other ultimate truth of our human condition, which is the fact that we begin with an inherited understanding that we can never completely abandon.

---

66. Luke 5:37-39.

Socrates and Jesus are the great masters who can hold these two truths together. They acknowledge and honor the foundational truth from which they began, and which remains the basis for most of their social interaction with others, but both point toward that greater truth toward which they are drawn.

CHAPTER SIX

Determinism, the Hermeneutic Circle, and Authenticity

OUR RECENT HISTORY has led us to believe that our human existence is far more determined than we had previously imagined. Our increased knowledge of genetics has convinced us that so much of what makes us the unique selves that we are is determined by codes within our DNA. Of course, not everything is determined by our DNA. Modern psychology tells us that much of who we are is determined by our earliest experiences, which we record on an unconscious level. That unconscious mind, which directs and determines so much of our lives, operates below the level of our conscious awareness and therefore beyond our control. Many believe that by the age of four the self that we become is already determined. If that isn't enough, beyond our formative years psychological conditioning and socialization continue to mold and shape us until there appears to be nothing left of human freedom.

In that same recent history, however, insights into our human condition have revealed a freedom previously unknown. This new-found freedom does not involve the facticity of our lives but the meaning we make of those facts. In the past, we believed that either the mind was a *tabula rasa* that simply recorded data as given, or that if the mind processed information it did so with a God-given active intellect (Thomas Aquinas) or a native hardware (Kant). Today, we know that the mind does process information but it does so with an understanding that is largely the product of human judgments and conventions passed onto us by our culture, history, and language communities. Certainly, there is some native hardware with which we are born but most of the understanding through which we process the data of our experience comes from human rather than divine or natural sources.

The fact that the understanding we inherit and through which we initially interpret the world is acquired uncritically at an early age seems to further support the determined nature of our existence, but the fact that it is the product of past human conventions and judgment attests to a freedom at its core. As we have seen, our history is full of individuals who re-conceptualized the world. We may inherit their understanding as our foundational orientation through which we interpret our experience, but what we really inherit is their second truth, that is, the new understanding they came to by rejecting their inherited understanding and taking on a new conceptual perspective.

This recent insight into our human condition illumines a freedom previously known only by a few. Now that we have come to realize that our initial orientation to the world originated as the second truths of individuals or groups of individuals, we are free, as never before, to pursue second truths of our own. Thus, although the circumstances or facts of our lives may be determined, our understanding, and thus interpretation, of those circumstances is freer than ever before.

It is, however, a freedom that is not open to everyone. Very young children are certainly excluded from participation in this freedom, and well they should be, for, as we have seen, at an early age what we need are foundational truths that are understood to be certain. The psychological health and wellbeing of children require a sense that the world is safe and predictable. At a certain age, however, it is beneficial to begin to introduce the child to alternative understandings. If this doesn't happen and the child's foundational orientation is too rigidly imposed, to the exclusion of any alternative understanding, the child may never realize the potential freedom that is also part of our human condition. This is why Einstein is reported to have said that if you want your children to be smart have them read fairytales, and if you want them to be really smart have them read more fairytales. Fairytales open young minds to the possibility of things being other than the way we have been taught to interpret them. This creates a very different kind of smart. It is not the smartness that we need to record our foundational understanding quickly, accurately, and uncritically but it is the kind of smart that advances our civilization and authenticates us as more than just members of the herd.

Part of the genius of Einstein was that he knew that physical reality went way beyond our understanding. He knew that the vastness of the universe far exceeded what we commonly knew and, therefore, he was able to imagine things yet unseen. For example, we know that the density of the earth, sun, and moon creates different gravitational forces and thus different escape velocities. In order to escape the earth's gravitational force an object has to move in excess of seven miles per second or 25,000 miles per hour. The escape velocity of the moon is much less, and the escape velocity of the sun is much more. Einstein imagined that in the vastness of the universe there must be masses so dense that their escape velocity would exceed the speed of light and thus no light could escape from the gravitational pull of that mass. Years later we found physical evidence to support what Einstein had imagined and the existence of black holes was confirmed. Einstein's genius lay in his imagination, that is, the ability to think about things differently than he had been taught to think about them. What if a straight line is not the shortest distance between two points? What if a curved line or geodesic is the shortest distance between two points? How would that alter our interpretation of reality? The genius of Einstein was not that he discovered new facts about the universe, but that he came to think about the universe differently. Einstein understood that reality always exceeds the understanding through which we interpret it, and therefore our understanding must change in order to take in more of that reality.

Of course, we cannot do this until a certain age. Children need to believe that their initial orientation to the world is certain, but at a certain age we want them to be open to a second truth and the kind of intelligence that the pursuit of a second truth requires. Such a pursuit demands more than mere intelligence, however. It also requires courage in that we are no longer supported by a truth that had promised us certainty. Additionally, there must be a hope and faith that a better interpretation always exists if we are open to having our conceptual perspective changed.

Up until we set out upon a journey in search of a second truth or better way to interpret things, we can only see what our understanding allows us to see. The truth of our understanding is what says "yes" or "no," "true" or "false" to the data of our experience. We interpret as true the data which conforms to our understanding and we reject the data which does not. Once we no longer trust that initial understanding, however, we open ourselves to the possibility of data that exceeds our understanding. Thus, we allow for possible experiences that our previous understanding eliminated. We begin to see and imagine things that we never saw or imagined before because they were simply blocked from our view by our understanding.

Narrow mindedness is largely a matter of rejecting data that does not conform to our understanding. Many people believe that critical thinking is no more than rejecting or being critical of ideas that do not conform to that understanding, but genuine critical thinking is much more a matter of being critical of the understanding through which we filter the data of our experience. Thus, open mindedness is a matter of exposing ourselves to a variety of different perspectives so that our foundational orientation loses some of its authority. Consequently, when we become open rather than closed minded, the data of our experience begin to shape our understanding rather than our understanding shaping the data of our experience.

This process is referred to as the hermeneutic circle, or perhaps it would be better termed the hermeneutic spiral, which is a very different kind of thinking. Normally, our understanding serves to filter our experience and only admits that data that conforms to it, but with the hermeneutic circle the process is just the reverse. Instead of insisting that the data conform to our understanding, we allow the data to do violence to our understanding and therefore open ourselves to the possibility of our understanding changing. Of course, we don't do this with all data and most of the time our understanding filters our experience in ways that allow us to function without much reflection. With some people this is their only mode of thought, but more creative types have a capacity to allow certain data to change the understanding through which they interpret their experience. Once our understanding is changed, we are open to new data that was previously filtered-out by our earlier understanding.

There is much more data than our understanding can process. Consider how different our experience would be if we could see like a hawk, hear like a dog, and smell like a bear. We would obviously experience a very different world. There may be little we can do to change the natural hardware through which we interpret the world, although the inventions of the telescope and microscope did do just that. The effect was that our understanding enormously changed to accommodate the new data. The same thing can be accomplished, however, by decreasing the understanding through which the data is processed. We do this, not by removing our inherited understanding, but by simply devaluing it to the point that we can imagine other alternative conceptualizations. Many people find such philosophical thinking difficult but in an age when we have become aware of the many factors that determine our existence, it may be our only source of real freedom.

Human beings are free in comparison to other creatures and even in comparison to our own ancestors, because we now know that the concepts through which we interpret our experience are not given by God or nature, but are largely the product of human judgments and conventions we inherit from past generations. Our realization of this affords us the freedom to assess, critique, and alter that inherited understanding. Past generations may have imagined that our conceptual hardware was natural or God-given but that is hard to maintain today with what we know about historicism, cultural relativism, and the nature of language. With such knowledge we are free, as never before, to reject such an inheritance, or at least to hold it loosely and create for ourselves ever new conceptual ways to interpret our experience. The reality of our human condition is that in spite of whatever genetic or environmental factors may determine our behavior, there is also always present the potential for a second truth or alternative conceptualization.

The way this happens is through a dialogue, but the interlocutor in *this* dialogue is the data of our experience. The data serve as the antithesis, which reveals the insufficiency of the understanding that is trying to process the data. Just as the interlocutor in a dialogue points out what is wrong with our understanding, so too does the data of our experience if we are open to having our understanding changed. At first this might seem to be just as deterministic as our genes or environment, but we get to choose what books we read and what people and activities we spend time with. Of course, we can read books and associate with people who simply confirm the prejudices of our inherited orientation, or we can choose to read books and associate with people who will challenge and perhaps alter that understanding. The intellectual and spiritual journey is always a matter of the latter.

This is the path less travelled. The path more travelled always insists that the data conform to the understanding and if it does not, it is rejected. The path more travelled is the path of the religious leaders who opposed Jesus or the path of the political leaders who opposed Nelson Mendela or Martin Luther King. Such people believed that truth was determined by its conformity to their foundational understanding; they were not completely wrong in believing that. We could not function as the kind of social creatures that we are if we did not have the ability to determine quickly and consistently whether something was true or not. A foundational truth that is open to change would not be very effective since its purpose is to assess something as true or false by its conformity to that understanding. This is part of our rational nature and it is essential that we be able to discriminate among the mass of data that comes our way as social creatures. People without this ability are deemed mentally ill or at least socially awkward. If, however, that is our only truth, then we are trapped within the understanding we inherit, and we will never be those unique individuals who authenticate themselves and equally provide the potential for the advance of civilization. In order to authenticate ourselves we need to exercise our freedom and be open to the data of our experience changing the understanding through which we interpret that experience. That is the nature of the understanding that we pursue in our intellectual or spiritual journeys. It is a truth that is always open to change.

Most people find little in the way of an authentic understanding for themselves because they were never told of a second truth or prepared through education to pursue it. We tell them to think outside the box, but so much of our educational system is about keeping everyone *inside* the box. Thinking outside the box is the openness to new interpretations because we allow the data to change our conceptual perspective. Sadly, almost all of our educational experiences reinforce rather than challenge our understanding.

Certainly, our educational system must provide solid foundations for the psychological health and wellbeing of the young. That is also beneficial in order to produce a socially cohesive society, but it does not produce authentic free thinkers who can advance our civilization. At some point our educational system must introduce and encourage students to be open to a second truth. Unfortunately, even on the graduate level, our education is largely about reinforcing a foundational understanding. Most graduate education is focused on ensuring that someone has been initiated into the specific understanding of a certain discipline or field. It provides the foundational understanding of a specific field, just as our early education provided a foundational understanding for social life in general. I once had a colleague who had a Ph.D. and could tell you what everyone in his field thought, but never had an original thought of his own. What he had been given is the foundational understanding that allowed him to speak and function within a certain social community or academic discipline, but he was not taught or encouraged to direct his thinking toward the second truth of his own authentic conceptual perspective.

The foundational nature of what is taught in the sciences is even worse. In the hard sciences, professionals are given strict methods and guidelines from which no one can veer without being excommunicated from the community. I know that we have to protect the young from the free exchange of ideas that could undermine their need for stable foundations, but when in our educational system do we stop just providing more foundational truths and introduce them to the idea of a second truth? Our educational institutions may speak of teaching critical thinking but they fail to see how deep that goes and what it really means to think outside the box.

We easily see religion as holding us back from pursuing a second truth, but it is also our educational and scientific institutions which equally insist upon a single foundational truth. Of course, many religious institutions have additional support for their foundational truth by claiming it to be God-given. If their understanding came directly from God, who does not change, they are never in need of a second truth. They may be right in that God does not change but the human interpretation of the divine revelation certainly does change, and for two reasons. First, we can only take in as much of the divine revelation as our understanding will allow, and the experience of a Divinity that is both infinite and eternal requires that our understanding must constantly expand. Second, if we are to have personal experiences with that which is holy and divine, as many people claim to have today, our understanding has to constantly change since that is the nature of a personal relationship. Anyone who says that after forty years of marriage they have the same understanding through which to interpret their spouse's behavior as on the day they married has no idea of who that other person is. One might have an idealized image of that other person but they cannot claim to have a personal and intimate relationship with them. Personal and intimate relationships demand that our understanding changes with our experience of them.

In the early books of the Judeo/Christian scripture the people believed that the Divinity that communed with them was their God and not the God of the whole earth. Certainly, he was not the god of the people on the other side of the river. The theologians of the Reformation and Counter-Reformation believed that the sun went around the earth. That is no longer our interpretation because our understanding has changed. Likewise, we no longer believe that the mind is a *tabula rasa* that simply records data as given. Twenty-first century people find it hard to believe in theologians who thought that the sun did go around the earth, and that their theologies were the direct result of what they saw in the biblical text. Of course, there are educated people today who do defend such theologies, but in most cases they are unaware or otherwise deny the interpretive nature of our human experience. They read books to strengthen and reinforce their presuppositions and prejudices rather than to challenge them, and they read their sacred texts through an equally sacredly held understanding.

Christian leaders seldom tell their congregations to allow the things that Jesus says and does in the Gospels to reform their socially accepted prejudices. Rather, they most often want their congregations to trust the understanding that the church gives them, to trust the theological perspective they are given to interpret the sacred text rather than allowing congregants their own experience with the text. Trusting your own reading of a sacred text as a unique experience that can change your understanding is very different than trusting the understanding and thus interpretation that religious leaders provide. Herein is the difference between people on spiritual journeys and people who simply trust a religious tradition. It is the difference between people who are looking for new and better ways to interpret their experience, and those who seek security by imagining a particular understanding is sacred.

In the twentieth century we saw not only the rise of fascism, totalitarianism, positivism, and fundamentalism, but also the existential and postmodern reactions to such sacredly held truths. These two opposing trends represent the two truths at the base of our human condition. Unfortunately, most of us believe there is only one truth, so we take sides and declare ourselves fundamentalists or existentialists—conservatives or liberals. A 21st century perspective concerning these two truths of the human condition, however, should put things in a better context. In order for that to happen, however, our educational, religious, and scientific institutions must do a much better job of teaching us how to move between these two truths and therein realize our full capacity for both reason and freedom.

CHAPTER SEVEN

Conservatives, Liberals, and a Security beyond our Own Understanding

I TEACH AT A CHRISTIAN COLLEGE where I have often argued that no two professors have the same theology, although two professors came pretty close. Both had gone to the same college at roughly the same time, had the same professors, and read the same books. I often think that when people disagree with me it's simply because they haven't read the books that I have read. Likewise, I find that whoever agrees with me on many points has read many of the same books that I've read. That is not completely true, since we can read books either with a mind that is open to new perspectives that expand our horizons or we can read the same book with a mind set upon finding ways to criticize those perspectives in order to defend the truth of our own perspective. That, by the way, is the difference between a liberal and conservative education. Conservative education is basically about learning how to apologetically defend the truth of our understanding, while liberal education is about exposing us to data that has the capacity to change our understanding.

In our early education we are given books that reinforce our foundational orientation. Our liberal education can only begin later when we feel secure enough that we no longer need to cling so tightly to the understanding through which we interpret our experience. That understanding provides an anchor for our identity until we are ready for an intellectual or spiritual journey. But even when we set out on such a journey the anchor stays with us and we are able to utilize it whenever needed. Part of wisdom is a matter of knowing when to anchor our thinking in our foundational understanding and utilize one mode of thought, and when to weigh anchor and utilize another mode of thinking in search of a better understanding. An ideally educated person is able to do both and knows how and when to move from one mode of thought to the other. Sadly, most people do not learn how to do this and become either conservative thinkers or liberal thinkers.

Many factors lie behind why we choose to lean one way or the other, but certainly the degree to which we look to knowledge for security is one. Young children live in a very confusing world because they don't know how anything works. Our early, non-critical education was largely a matter of being taught how to make sense of our experience by adults passing their conceptual understanding on to us. It is quite natural for us to identify that understanding with truth itself. At a later age, however, when that understanding is overwhelmed by data that we can no longer process, we can be tempted to fall into one of two extremes. Either, we can give up on all truth and become nihilists, or we can try to salvage our understanding by destroying the data and whoever presents it. Neither extreme is a good solution. It is much better that as we mature intellectually and spiritually we loosen our identification with our first truth and begin to embrace the idea that the ultimate truth is something much greater than our understanding, and therefore our understanding must constantly change as we pursue that greater truth.

In the past, when we were unaware of the interpretive nature of our human experience, the need to constantly change our understanding was not apparent. Throughout most of history people were surrounded by others who had the same understanding and interpreted things in such a similar way that it was easy to imagine that our experience was simply given rather than an interpretation. For long periods of human history few people read, and there were very few books to be read. I remember being told that there was a time in human history when a private individual could actually own all the books in the world. It was a time shortly after the invention of the printing press, which made books affordable. Prior to that time only royalty could afford to own all the books in the world. It wasn't long after the invention of the printing press, however, that there were simply too many books for any individual to own all of them.

With so many books available, unanimity concerning our understanding became ever more difficult to achieve and maintain, although in rural communities, where everyone went to the same church, did the same kind of work, and read little, unanimity happened and was maintained without much effort. Without being exposed to other perspectives, one may easily assume that one's own understanding is a universal truth shared by everyone. Additionally, the mass media of the 20th century also contributed to establishing and maintaining the illusion that our understanding was much more than a particular perspective since it was being shared by nearly everyone we knew. With more and more people having their understanding molded by television rather than the great diversity of views available from books, it is easy to see how a perspective shared by so many people could come to be seen as a universal truth. That, along with the ever-present peer pressure to conform rather than stand out, reinforced the truth of our common understanding.

The internet of the 21st century has countered that trend, however, and we are now faced with a greater diversity of understanding than the world has ever seen. Change is happening at an enormously rapid rate because the free exchange of ideas is freer than it has ever been. Today, with internet publishing, blogs, and books on demand, everyone can publish and share their unique understanding without fear of being ostracized or burned alive as heretics. Today, there are many more than the original three television networks in the U.S., as well as an enormous number of internet videos. These are the kinds of developments that make for changes in historical epochs. The change from the medieval world to the modern world was essentially a matter of the world having gotten so much bigger because of inventions like the microscope and telescope, and the discovery of the new world. The world was presenting us with new data and our understanding had to change in order to make sense of that data. Of course, those who overly identified their understanding as *the* truth resisted such change. Sometimes the resistance was violent and they thought their violence justified because they were defending *the* truth.

Even those who welcome a new understanding, however, are often quick to make it into the new sacred truth. True science, however, like true spirituality, must always be based on an understanding that is provisional and open to accommodate new data. Sadly, throughout much of the history of both science and religion that has not been the case. Conservatives and liberals alike have, for the most part, insisted upon our experience conforming to what they take to be a sacred understanding. We find it hard to accept the fact that all of our theories are provisional and any claim beyond that is blasphemous because it attempts to reduce a divine creation to something that can be comprehensively known by us.

Of course, if we equate our understanding with divine truth it does give us a sense of security, albeit a false sense. Regrettably, it is common for religious people to do just that and find security in the firmness of their own understanding. The results of that equation have been disastrous. Christian history is full of Catholics killing Protestants, Protestants killing Catholics, and both burning heretics alive in the name of Jesus. At the base of the violence is the idea that there is one and only one truth, and those that possess that truth have the right to kill those who do not possess it. As we have seen, however, in terms of our human understanding there are really two truths, and the second truth, as people like Socrates and Jesus conceptualize it, is something that we never possess but rather something that possesses us.

All great spiritual teachers present us with a perspectival understanding that is very diffe rent from the common view. That is true of great intellectual figures as well but we have a much easier time grasping their second truth because they are speaking about their experience with the world, which is common to us all, but great spiritual teachers are speaking of their experience with the divine, which is not common to us all. Most people are so distracted by their experience of the world that they are unable to recognize the small, still, silence of the Divine. Thus, the things that great spiritual teachers speak of are unfamiliar to us. Consequently, we usually pick out what is familiar from what the spiritual teacher says and build our interpretation around that.

The common notion among Christians is that Jesus' teachings are about love, but Jesus' understanding of the Divine goes much deeper than that. In fact, Jesus tells us that our idea of love is misconceived and misdirected. It is not that we lack love, but that our love is misdirected and almost exclusively focused on what we misconceive as *our own*. So much of the evil in the world comes from the fact that we love our own country, our own family, our own life, our own reputation, and our own truth so much that if anyone does harm to anyone or anything that is our own, we respond with violence and destruction. This is why Jesus says, "If anyone comes to me and does not hate father and mother, wife and children, brothers and sisters—yes, even their own life—such a person cannot be my disciple."[67] Jesus reminds us that nothing is our own—everything is God's—but we choose to love only that portion of God's creation that we imagine is our own, and therein is the evil that keeps us from a deeper knowledge and intimacy with the Divine.

---

67. Luke 14:26

Certainly we want a loving god, but we want our god to love the way we love; that is, we want a god to love what is ours and not love what does harm to ours. Jesus' teachings, however, present us with a creator who loves all of creation as we love our own family, country, or lives. We are able to extend mercy and forgiveness to our children even when they do things that hurt us because we see them as ours, but the Divinity that Jesus reveals is able to extend mercy and forgiveness to the whole of creation, while our mercy and forgiveness is limited to what we consider our own, and not to those that do harm to our own.

A colleague, Dan, told me a story about his experience of growing up without a father. He told me that he had a friend whose father was very active in his son's life, and the man would include Dan in many of the activities he did with his son. As time went on, and as Dan's attachment to his friend's father grew he came to the painful realization that this man would never love Dan in the same way he loved his son. This would seem obvious and natural to most, but Dan told me, "I always thought there was something evil about that." He went on to say, "The only way it wouldn't be evil was if there was a father who loved everyone the same."

I once told that story to someone who told me that Dan was ungrateful and that his friend's father was good and not evil. Certainly that is true when compared to other fathers who pay no attention to those that are not their sons or daughters, but not in comparison to a Divinity that loves all of creation. Of course, that is not the kind of divinity we want to know. Indeed, perhaps only the marginalized, the orphaned, or the fatherless can know such a Divinity. The rest of us want a god that loves what is our own and hates what does harm to our own.

People do not take Jesus' teaching about loving our enemies seriously because they fail to see the evil in loving our own and hating those that do harm to our own. I often present a thought experiment in class that riles everyone, and I am sure it will rile the reader as well. I tell my students that if this was really a Christian nation, and George Bush was really a Christian, he would have gotten on TV after 9/11 and said to the terrorists, "Whatever we did to anger you this much, please forgive us, and we certainly forgive you." Christians believe that Jesus takes the guilt of the world upon himself, suffers it without retaliation, and says, "It is finished."[68] The evil ends when the innocent suffer the offense without retaliation and offer forgiveness in exchange for violence. Jesus tells us to pick up our cross and follow him into the same kind of forgiveness that he models, but we are unable to follow him into that forgiveness because we love too much what we imagine is our own.

Now this is just a thought experiment and I know George Bush could not have done that. Even Christian pastors in this country would have run him out of office, but it should show us how short we fall from following Jesus and taking his teachings seriously because we fail to see the evil in loving our own. In those rare causes where it is done, however, we see a divine power that cripples the earthly power of violence. Whenever we see an innocent suffer violence and respond with forgiveness rather than retaliation (e.g., Gandhi, Mandela, and Martin

---

68. John 19:30.

Luther King), we recognize a divine holiness that is out of reach for most of us because we love our own and hate those who do harm to what we consider our own. Those individuals whom I have met who do love their enemies more genuinely than others are usually people who have given up on the idea that anything is their own and therefore they have eliminated the possibility of having enemies. Buddhists also are taught to eliminate attachments. Such people are able to take seriously the teaching that tells us that "If anyone would sue you and take your coat, let him have your cloak as well."[69] I'm sure many Buddhists follow such teachings of Jesus as devoutly as Christians.

This is often very hard for people who live in a capitalist society to hear. We are told that life is all about increasing what is our own, so we create theologies that make Jesus, and so many other great spiritual teachers who said similar things, into something we can live with instead of allowing their teachings to change our perspectival understanding.

Of course, it is not an easy matter to change our perspective and come to see that nothing is our own. We love believing that we have security in the things we possess, and of all the things we possess perhaps our greatest source of security comes from our understanding. This is true even of poor people who have little in the way of material possessions but find security in the fact that they possess an understanding that they equate with the one and only truth. This is true of liberals as well as conservatives. Liberals may be open to a new perspective but once that new perspective is formed they too come to find security

---

69. Matthew 5:40.

in believing they are in possession of *the* truth. To live in the liminal space of a forever provisional understanding is difficult and leaves us without the kind of firm understanding that provides others with a sense of certainty. In the absence of such an understanding, however, great spiritual teachers often speak of another source of security that comes from a deep sense that someone or something is holding on to them and they are perfectly safe, even without the security that others derive from clinging to their understanding and imagining it as sacred.

Throughout the Platonic dialogues, Socrates speaks of his *daemon* who faithfully tells him when he is going astray. Socrates is always suspicious of his own understanding but he trusts a benevolent spirit that he recognizes as greater than himself. A trust in something greater than ourselves gave us our first experience of feeling secure. Even before we had developed an understanding from which to glean a sense of security, the arms of loving parents provided that sense. Our personal experience with the Divine can also give us that same sense of being held and feeling safe. Traditional religion, at least in the West, has not done a very good job of leading us into such an experience that can provide us with that kind of security. They told us that there was a God who loved us but we only had access to that love by performing certain rituals, believing certain doctrines, or practicing some moral code. They tried to assure us that there was a God who was willing to love us but the Divine was like us and loved some more than others based upon how well they matched up to the standards that a specific religion provided. Thus, they provided us with a security that came from the belief that we knew how things worked, but that is very different from the initial security that comes from being held in a parent's arms.

Jesus tells us that we should think of God as a heavenly father, and although nearly all versions of Christianity have been faithful to a parental image of God, it is usually the image of a disciplining parent who rewards and punishes in order to mold our behavior. Jesus, however, presents us with a very different parental image. He tells us that unless we become as little children we will not enter the kingdom of heaven.[70] "Little children" or perhaps better "infants" have a different parental experience. It is the primary experience of a parent's arms and the security that comes from that experience which produces the heavenly state of which Jesus speaks. Of course, most forms of Christianity have made Jesus' reference to heaven into some future state of reward for right thinking or right behaving rather than the state of consciousness that comes from the experience of the divine presence. That experience is not encountered through either the first truth or the second truth but through the pre-linguistic and ineffable consciousness of an infant in its parent's arms.

All too quickly, we leave that infantile state and acquire an inherited understanding that replaces our parents' arms as our source of security. As we have seen, in some people that inherited understanding eventually gives way to a quest for a second truth. With some their second truth is little different from their inherited truth and it simply replaces their inherited understanding as their source of security. What Socrates and Jesus reveal,

---

70. Matthew 18:3.

however, is that the best among us are able to live in a liminal space where their security comes not by them holding tightly to a particular understanding but from a deep sense that something is holding onto them. Socrates finds his security in a benevolent spirit who he trusts rather than his own understanding, and Jesus in a loving heavenly Father. Jesus says he does nothing out of his own understanding "but only what he sees the Father doing."[71] What we see with both Socrates and Jesus is that their sense of security comes from the experience of a benevolent presence greater than their own.

The fact that our conceptual understanding changes over time (both for us as individuals and as a species) should tell us that it is a poor source of security. The creative nature of human beings demands that the understanding through which we interpret the world must be fluid, but more importantly, if it is not seen as fluid it all too easily comes to be seen as sacred and consequently a source of evil. These were the people who killed both Socrates and Jesus, and such people continue to feel justified in killing people who do not embrace their sacred understanding.

To believe that our understanding represents God's eternal truth is both naïve and blasphemous, especially for Christians who follow one who said, "I am the way, and the truth, and the life."[72] The ultimate truth of our human condition is a way or path that we are to follow. In fact, the early followers of Jesus did not refer to themselves as Christians but as followers of

---

71. John 5:19.
72. John 14:6.

The Way.[73] I take this quite literally and think that the ultimate truth concerning our understanding is the Jesus perspective, and once we begin to see how radically divine that perspective is, we should equally realize that it is a perspective that we will never fully possess but one that we humbly pursue. It is hard to imagine that people could realistically believe that they have the Jesus perspective. In order to fully take on the Jesus perspective we would have to shed all of the cultural, historical, and linguistic prejudices that make up our inherited understanding (both on the conscious and unconscious level). That is clearly impossible but it should be the ambition of Christians to allow the things that Jesus said and did to undermine our own understanding in order to bring us ever closer to the Jesus perspective. The Jesus perspective is the ultimate truth that Christians should be seeking and as they come ever closer to that ultimate truth they have an ever better perspectival understanding through which to read all of Scripture.

---

73. Acts 9:2.

CHAPTER EIGHT

Reading Sacred Scriptures through the Two Truths

AS WE HAVE SEEN, people on intellectual or spiritual journeys are always working with two understandings and therefore many of their concepts have more than a single meaning. If it is an intellectual journey, they have the traditional concepts of their discipline, but also the personal concepts that are unique to them. If it's a spiritual journey, they have traditional notions of things like sin, righteousness, and God, but they also have the personal concepts that their unique journey has shaped. An authentic intellectual or spiritual journey forces us to live between these two conceptual understandings: one that we no longer see as sacred but we continue to use in order to communicate with others, and a second understanding which remains open and therefore we never fully grasp.

Socrates is a great example of such a life. He honors and cherishes his Athenian foundations to the point that he is willing to die rather than undermine that foundational understanding. In Plato's *Crito*, Socrates' student, Crito tries to convince Socrates to let his students help him escape the death sentence that he is under. Socrates' response is amazing. He refuses to escape his death sentence because he says he would be undermining the laws of Athens. He asks Crito,

> Suppose that while we were preparing to run away from here—or however one should describe it—the laws and constitution of Athens should come and confront us and ask this question, Now, Socrates, what are you proposing to do? Can you deny that by this act which you are contemplating you intend, so far as is in your power, to destroy us, the laws, and the whole of the state as well? . . . . How shall we answer this question, Crito?[74]

Socrates goes on to say that since he had no problem with the law and the whole of Athenian culture that gave him his foundational truth, why should he have problems with it now simply because it sentences him to death? That reaction of Socrates always struck me as strange and very different from the way most human beings would respond, but it is part of Socratic wisdom. Socrates knows that he could never have been Socrates in any other place but Athens. Only the Athenian culture and the foundational understanding it provided could support Socrates and his specific quest for a second truth.

The situation is even more striking with Jesus. He too honors the understanding he inherits from a cultural and religious tradition that told of individuals' encounters with God and how they interpreted those encounters. That tradition established the basis for Jesus' initial orientation and his own relationship with

---

74. Plato, *Crito,* 50a4-b5.

the Divine. That inherited understanding, however, was subordinated to a deeper understanding that came out of his constant awareness of a Divine presence that he referred to as his father and our father. Thus, like Socrates, he acknowledges and affirms his inherited understanding, while pointing beyond it as well.

The data of our experience has the power to change our inherited understanding if we no longer hold it to be sacred. This is especially true regarding the data that comes through our experience with the Divine. This insight should be helpful when dealing with what otherwise appears to be inconsistencies within the Scripture and especially the Gospels. For example, from its inception, Christianity has had to deal with the fact that although Jesus presents a picture of God very different from the often angry God of the Jewish Scriptures, he constantly confirms the truth of those Scriptures and their divine origin. The ancient Christian church tried to solve the problem by reading what came to be known as the Old Testament allegorically in order to make it consistent with what Jesus said and did. That was probably a better solution than the modern, more literal reading of the reformers who claimed that both were objectively true and God was both loving and just. Hence, theologies developed that explained how God could be both merciful and just at the same time. He was just and wrathful toward some but merciful and loving toward others who had said the magic words, practiced the right rituals, or perfected their behavior or doctrines. Such a theology can be attractive since it gives us the ability to find favor with God and equally condemn those people whose rituals, behaviors, or doctrines are different from our own. According to such a theology, when Jesus tells us to love our enemies, he must mean those enemies in our own tribe who have found favor with God and not those enemies on the other side of the river who have not found favor and are under God's wrath. This gives us the liberty to love our enemies who are like us but at the same time kill those enemies who are not like us.

It is a quite different situation if we believe that God is the God of the whole earth and extends mercy because of who God is and not because of something that we do or do not do. If we take that position, how do we make sense of the striking difference between the God of the Old Testament and the picture of God that Jesus presents? If we read things through the two truths, however, we can see how Jesus can both confirm the Jewish Scripture and at the same time have a very different view of God from what is often put forth in the Scripture. Anyone who has their identity founded upon a vital relationship with the Divine has experienced their understanding changing over time because of that relationship. In fact, if our conceptual understanding does not change, it means either we do not have a relationship with the Divine or that we have such trust in our own understanding that even our encounters with a Divine presence cannot unseat or alter that understanding, because it rather than God is sacred. That was certainly the case with the religious leaders of Jesus' day; even their encounter with a divine presence could not unseat their faith in their own understanding. This is still the nature of many religious people today.

Anyone on a spiritual journey must remain open to having their understanding changed by their encounters with the

Divine. That, however, is only part of what is being revealed in a sacred text like the Bible. The other part is that people's first encounter with the Divine is almost always interpreted through their foundational orientation, rather than the second truth that they are being drawn into. The God that is revealed in Scripture always meets people in their foundational understanding, only then to reveal that the Divine is more than they imagine. Thus, their initial interpretation of their experience with the Divine is always a misinterpretation because of their misunderstanding of who God is.

We all begin our relationship with the Divine by either imagining who we would be if we were God or from an inherited understanding passed onto us from others. Those are the only understandings we are capable of in our initial God experience, but the nature of the Divinity that is revealed in almost all sacred Scriptures is a God who patiently works with our initial orientation in order to slowly bring us to a better understanding and deeper intimacy. In the early revelations recorded in the Judeo/Christian Scripture most of the Biblical characters interpreted their God experiences tribally: that is, that this Divinity was the God of their own people and not the god of people who had different beliefs, rituals, and behaviors. Initially, everyone interprets their God experience through their own culture, history, and language community. That is unavoidable, yet somehow many people today believe that the Biblical revelation is an objective revelation rather than people's interpretation of their God experiences. Such a view of sacred Scripture is especially unrealistic given what we now know about the nature of our human condition and how we experience everything, including God. Perhaps it was natural to view the Scripture as an objective revelation when we believed that human experience was objective, but now that we know of the interpretive nature of all of our experience, it is realistic to see Scripture as a divine revelation of our interpretations of our God experiences. As such, it is still a divine revelation but what is revealed is human beings, interpretation or misinterpretation of their experiences with the Divine. All intimate communication is of this nature since the one desiring the intimacy wants to be known more deeply, which requires that the one to whom they are communicating change their understanding. In the Biblical revelation God is depicted as patiently and mercifully communing with human beings in spite of their misunderstanding in the hope of bringing them to a better understanding in order that they might become more divine themselves.

There has long been the question of whether the Scripture is divinely inspired, but the more interesting question is what is God revealing in the divine revelation? I knew a professor who as an undergraduate had four different Bible professors who all believed that the Bible was divinely inspired, but all believed something different. Among the diversity of opinions, one of the more common views concerning divine inspiration was greatly influenced by early modern science, which purported that truth should be objective, certain, and precise after the model of mathematics. If that is our concept, then the truth that is being revealed in Scripture is objective, certain, and precise. Of course, that is to read the Scripture through a modern, scientific concept, but if the Divine is personal and desires intimate relationships with human beings, a more realistic understanding of Scripture would be as a record of those relationships with none of our warts or misunderstandings removed.

Certainly, the God that is depicted in the Judeo/Christian Scripture does desire to correct our misunderstandings. All personal, intimate relationships are of this nature. We come to know others intimately by allowing our understanding of them to be changed through our experience with them, and if our understanding does not change over time that is evidence that it is not an intimate relationship. The same is true of our relationship with the Divine. God begins speaking to us long before we can really understand. That is the only way that communication can begin. All deep communication begins in misunderstanding, but misunderstanding is still an understanding, and the only one we have at the beginning. Some of our relationships never get much beyond that initial misunderstanding, but some of our experiences with others change our understanding of them and give us a deeper and more intimate way to interpret our experience with them. This is the nature of our personal relationship with the Divine, and it is the history of God's relationship with us as a species.

I recently met a woman who was teaching at a rabbinical college. She told me that semester she was teaching Leviticus. I cringed at the thought of teaching Leviticus, but she said that she loved teaching it because it was all black and white, good and bad, inside and outside. Everything was very simple. I asked what about the later books where God rebukes the people for doing to the stranger or outsider what earlier books presented as permissible and God ordained. She responded by saying, "Oh, you mean when morality developed." Certainly she didn't mean that there was no morality in the time of Leviticus but it certainly was a different morality than in the time of the prophets. God had become bigger in the prophets' understanding, and morality was extended beyond the tribe.

Initially, people want no more than a tribal God and God meets them there. In fact, people with a tribal morality would only worship a God who would help them kill their enemies. A God who would tell them to love their enemies would be incomprehensible. Indeed, today many religious people still cannot comprehend anything more than a tribal god. That is almost always the place of our initial encounter with the Divine, but the purpose behind divine communication is always to bring us to a deeper awareness of how different God is from what we imagine or from what we have been told.

This is the nature of the Biblical revelation. Abraham and Moses begin with a certain conception of who God is, but they feel called by God to go on journeys. The nature of their journey brings them into the unfamiliar, which requires that their understanding must change. If we never go on a journey our foundational orientation can sometimes last a lifetime, but a journey forces us to begin to seek a second truth that will make sense of our new experiences. With Abraham and Moses their new experiences change who they think God is and who they perceive themselves to be in relationship to God. The same is true of David, although his is more a spiritual rather than physical journey. David has a different concept of God after his experience with Bathsheba (adultery) and Uriah (murder) than before those experiences.

Our experiences with the Divine are meant to change our conceptual perspective, but sadly many people insist upon interpreting all experiences, including their God experiences, according to what they see as their own sacred perspective. By treating the understanding through which they interpret their God experiences as immutable and certain, they create the illusion that they are in the possession of absolute truth, but in reality the only thing that is immutable and certain is their own perspectival understanding.

This is typical of many religious people. They may claim that they have faith in a sacred text, but in fact their faith is very different from the kind of faith we find in most sacred texts. What is revealed in the Biblical text is a dynamic faith through which the Biblical characters' understanding of both God and themselves is changed. We might try to create an objective and immutable theology out of what we find in the Bible, but the Biblical characters themselves had a theology that was open to their God experiences. It was a theology that was ever-changing in order to draw them into a deeper interpretation and intimacy with God. All of the great Biblical characters end with a concept of God that is very different from the concept with which they began. Many religious people today do not like that idea. They want to believe that the truth is the truth; that it is fixed, certain, and unchanging, but that is not how we actually experience either truth or the Divine.

Nearly every major Biblical character, as well as the great figures throughout the history of the Christian church, introduces innovation to what had been the foundational truth with which they began. In order to do so they had to cherish the sacredness of their God experience and allow that experience to move them beyond the first truth of their initial orientation. Strangely, the religious people who later follow and accept the understanding the innovators created are very different from the innovators themselves. They cherish the foundational understanding they inherit but reject the idea that their own personal God experiences could change that inherited truth. Thus, although they say they are followers and have the same understanding, they are really talking about two very different truths. Those who introduce innovation concerning the way they think about God and their relationship to God are always dealing with a second truth, while their followers are always dealing with a foundational, first truth, even when they use the same words as the founders of their traditional understanding.

This fact that those who pursue a second truth are nothing like the defenders of foundational truths is the basis for the conflict between Jesus and the religious leaders of his day, and it is still the basis for conflict between religious leaders of today and those who wish to follow Jesus' example and pursue a second truth. The religious leaders of today tell us that men like Jesus, Augustine, Thomas, Francis, Luther, Calvin, and Wesley were the exceptions, and we should not follow their example, but instead trust the traditional understanding they have passed onto us rather than trusting our own God experiences as they did.

Most people's experience with organized religion has not taught them about a dynamic Biblical faith that promises to bring them into an ever-deeper concept of God and themselves, but rather presents them with a theological faith in a foundational truth that claims to be eternal and immutable. This is unavoidable since our human nature requires that our first truth or foundational understanding must be seen as absolute and certain in order to provide a firm basis for our psychological development and social wellbeing. Many people maintain and defend that foundational truth all of their lives and they see those in pursuit of a second truth as the enemy of their truth. All of our intellectual history can be read through this conflict, but it is especially illuminating if we bring this perspective to our reading of the Gospel.

Jesus and the Two Truths

Jesus has a foundational orientation that he shares with other Palestinian Jews of two thousand years ago, but there is a second truth that he is coming to out of his prayerful relationship with the Father. He, like so many other great historical figures, is working out of two very different conceptual contexts. Obviously, he interprets much of his experience as a result of the foundational orientation that he received as a Palestinian Jew during the time of the Roman occupation, but he is also having many of his concepts changed by his experiences in the Father presence. Like anyone on a spiritual journey, he is coming into a new understanding, although he never completely abandons the foundational orientation which was the basis from which his journey began and the basis from which he often communicates his ministry to others.

Consequently, when scholars insist upon contextual analysis and try to read the Gospel in the context of the Jewish culture of two thousand years ago, they get less than half the picture. Certainly that context is helpful, and many times Jesus is speaking out of and into that context, but more often he is speaking out of the context of someone who has spent so much time on a spiritual journey into the Divine presence that his conceptual understanding has been changed and is the unique and authentic result of that experience. Unlike other great historical figures, however, Jesus does not write long explanations of how his concepts have been changed by his experience and it is up to us to find them in all the radical things that Jesus says and does. We are helped in this effort if we are aware of the two truths that are always at work within anyone who has a genuine, dynamic relationship with the Divine.

Thus, in addition to everything else that Jesus offers, he also provides an ideal model for how to live between these two truths that are so much a part of our human condition. Jesus never dismisses the foundational truth that he inherits. It is the orientation into which his ministry often speaks and it was his own initial understanding that gave him a basis for his prayerful communion with the Divine. At other times, however, he is speaking out of a conceptual context that is very different from that of his culture and history. Consequently, Jesus can both confirm the law and at other times appear to be destroying the law, because he has such a different concept of law. Often, when he speaks to the religious leaders of his day he is speaking to how they conceptualize the law and the fear and dread it produced in them. At other times, however, he is speaking out of the unique understanding of law that has come out of his intimate connection with the Divine.

From reading the Gospel, I am convinced that no one has ever had their understanding changed as much by their spiritual journey as Jesus, but we should all have our conceptual understanding changed by our journey just as Jesus had. We all fall short of going as far on the journey as Jesus does and therefore none of us fully achieve the Jesus perspective because none of us are as constantly aware of the Divine presence as Jesus was. The distractions of the world are simply too much for us and we have our attention diverted from an awareness of the Divine presence in a way that Jesus' attention was never diverted.

The Spanish philosopher Ortega y Gasset (1883-1955) claimed that love was essentially a matter of attention abnormally fixed.[75] We give our attention to the ones we love and when we have a lack of attention toward someone they rightly interpret that as a lack of love. Unfortunately, human beings cannot give their attention to anything for very long. We are easily distracted, and only overcome those distractions when we fall in love. The experience of being "in love" is the experience of having our attention abnormally fixed upon another. Jesus apparently loved the experience of his Father's presence and practiced an awareness of that presence constantly. From the

75. Ortega y Gasset. *On Love.* 64.

things we read in the Gospels, it appears that the omnipresence of God was not a theory for Jesus but a constant experience from which he never diverted. From all that Jesus says and does it appears that he understood that God's ultimate desire was simply that we would fix our attention upon God as God's attention is always fixed upon us. Because of the things that Jesus says, I have come to think of prayer (with or without word) as simply our attention fixed upon God. This gives meaning to the Apostle Paul's admonition to "pray without ceasing."[76] Not that we are to constantly mumble words but that we are to be constantly aware of the Divine presence in every moment of our lives.

Of course, we are easily distracted from an awareness of that presence by all the things that Jesus speaks of in the Sermon on the Mount. As we mentioned earlier, he equates these distractions with sin and tells us that lust is the same as adultery and anger is the same as murder. He also warns us of other distractions like worry and earthly treasure[77] which easily capture our attention and keep us from an awareness of the Divine presence. These are our deeper sins that grieve God's heart, but whenever we return to a state of prayer and become once again mindful of that presence, we are always received into it through forgiveness and mercy. This is the concept of sin that Jesus puts forth in the Sermon on the Mount and much of the rest of the Gospel as well, but it is not Jesus' only understanding.

At other times, when dealing with people who were confident that they knew what sin was and would never accept

---

76. 1Thessalonians 5:17.
77. Matthew 5:1-7:17.

Jesus' radical concept of sin, he spoke out of the foundational understanding he shared with them. That is always the case with those individuals who are trying to introduce us to a new way to interpret our experience, but it is also true of many average individuals in today's advanced industrialized society.

Today, many business people, lawyers, doctors, or philosophers speak differently when addressing non-professionals than when speaking to colleagues in their field, or at least they should for the sake of good communication. The same is true of non-professionals whose familiarity with fly fishing, mountain biking, or stamp collecting takes them far beyond the common understanding in those areas. Our relationship with what we love most and spend most time with produces in us a perspectival understanding that is very different from what the average person has regarding that particular field of interest. Good communicators are aware of this and when dealing with those less versed in such areas, they communicate using concepts common to those of the general culture and language community. From the Gospel text, we can see that Jesus was a communicator who spoke out of these two very different understandings. When dealing with the religious leaders of his day he most often speaks out of the common understanding, but at other times he is speaking to people who are not locked into their own understanding but have "ears to hear"[78] what he is saying. At those times, he is speaking out of the very different conceptual context that has come about because of his unique, prayerful relationship with the Divine.

---

78. Matthew 11:15, 13:9, Mark 4:9.

As we have said, if we really want to know another person on that most intimate level, one of the things we want to know is how their unique experience has molded the understanding through which they try to make sense of their life. Authentic people, at some point, realize that the perspective they inherit is inadequate to account for their unique experience, and therefore they set out to create an understanding for themselves that provides a better interpretation of their experience. Jesus is an example of a most authentic human being whose conceptual orientation had been changed by his experience in the Divine presence. If we really wish to know Jesus, what we are really after is that authentic conceptual perspective. Indeed, our ultimate ambition should be to make the Jesus' perspective our own. In order to do so, we should read the Gospel with an eye to how unique his conceptual understanding is. When Jesus says things that do not make sense when read through a common understanding, what anyone who is serious about following Jesus should do is let those difficult things that Jesus says change their concepts in order that we interpret our experience closer to the way that Jesus interpreted his.

That is not the way most religious people read the Gospel. They read the things that Jesus says through a common understanding instead of trying to get to Jesus' unique perspective. That was certainly the way the religious leaders of Jesus' day interpreted the things he said, and that is still the way most religious people read his words today. When something that Jesus said does not conform to the common understanding, they ignore it or create theologies that explain how Jesus didn't really mean what he said. The reason they refuse to hear what Jesus says is often the same reason that the religious leaders of his day refused to hear him. It is because Jesus tells us we are not good and that God alone is good.[79]

It is common for human beings to think of themselves as good people. We know from our experience that human beings love good people and do not love bad people. Our desire to be loved causes us to want to think of ourselves as good people. We bring that understanding to our first experiences with the Divine and imagine that God must be like us, but Jesus tells us that God is nothing like us and divine love is not a response to some goodness within us but comes to us through God's forgiveness and mercy. That is the good news, but human beings have trouble interpreting that as good news. We want a god that loves in response to our righteousness and not out of forgiveness and mercy. Certainly, there is reason for this. Human society wants a god that reinforces good behavior and punishes bad behavior so we almost all begin with such a concept of god, and that might not be a bad place from which to begin; it is just not a good place to end. All wisdom begins with a fear of God,[80] but "perfect love casts out fear; …and whoever fears has not reached perfection in love."[81] These are the two truths concerning our understanding of God.

Of course, we are willing to accept the idea that for us there is nothing to fear in God, but not for all who find themselves

---

79. Mark 10:18, Luke 18:19.
80. Psalm 111:10, Prov. 1:7, Proverbs 9:10.
81. 1 John 4:18.

in need of mercy. In fact, the only way we can accept the idea of God's mercy is by qualifying it and insisting that asking for God's forgiveness and mercy must be done with the words, practices, or rituals that our theologies prescribe. We only love our own and only want forgiveness and mercy extended to our own. We take the Gospel—the greatest story ever told—and make it into abstract and objective theologies by which we can determine who gets to go to heaven and who goes to hell. It seems clear to me that Jesus knows that God extends the Divine, eternal presence to all who are willing to come into that presence through forgiveness. Jesus says, "No one comes to the Father except through me."[82] We have made theologies out of that, but Jesus never told us what that meant. Instead, he showed us what it meant from the cross. From the cross Jesus prays for his torturers to be forgiven, and he reveals to us the nature of divine forgiveness, whereby the innocent, offended one suffers the offense without retaliation in order to restore relationship with the guilty through forgiveness. What a beautiful picture of divine forgiveness, and every human being regardless of their beliefs, behaviors, or rituals come into eternal relationship with the Divine through that forgiveness and in no other way. That is the great revelation of the cross.

Sadly, both Catholic and mainline Protestant churches have interpreted the revelation of the cross as God responding to our sin by pouring forth his wrath upon Jesus. They insist that God is just and that someone must pay for the offense of our sin. The eleventh century theory of the atonement that stands as the

---

82. John 14:6.

official position of both Catholic and most Protestant churches claims that Jesus, the sinless one, took the sin of the world upon himself and therein suffered God's wrath in our place. Jesus does indeed take our sin upon himself but the cross is the picture not of a man suffering God's wrath but the picture of what divine forgiveness is all about. It is the Divine suffering the wrath of human beings and responding to it with forgiveness.

Justice requires that the guilty pay for their offense, so the idea that Jesus, the innocent one, suffering in place of guilty sinners does not satisfy a desire within God for justice. It is not justice when the innocent, offended party suffers an offense without retaliation or demand that the guilty pay for their offense, but forgiveness. In fact, that is the very nature of forgiveness and what makes it stand in direct opposition to the idea of justice. When harm is done someone must suffer but the question is who is to suffer? Justice requires that the guilty suffer, but with forgiveness the suffering is limited to the innocent by their desire to exonerate the guilty.

Justice never restores a relationship between the innocent and the guilty. It merely provides the innocent some satisfaction in knowing that the guilty were made to suffer as they suffered. Justice always adds more suffering to the world, and the only thing that ends suffering is forgiveness. Jesus says, "It is finished."[83] God's response to our sin ends in an act of forgiveness whereby the Divine suffers the offense without retaliation or demand that the guilty pay for the offense. Jesus prays for his torturers to be forgiven in order to restore relationship with

---

83. John 19:30.

them, but prayer is not enough as anyone who has ever forgiven a serious offense knows. The one who forgives must willingly suffer the offense without retaliation or demand for justice in order to restore relationship with the guilty party.

Imagine someone taking your credit card and charging $20,000 to it, and then asking you to forgive them. If you ask them to repay you the money in order for you to forgive them, you are asking for justice and not offering forgiveness. Real forgiveness is a matter of restoring relationship with the guilty by having the innocent alone pay for the offense, and therein vindicate the guilty party.

In terms of our sin, God is the offended party and the nature of forgiveness requires that the Divine suffer instead of the guilty in order to restore relationship with them. That is the beautiful picture of Jesus on the cross, but it is usually more than we are willing to accept about God, because it is more than we are willing to accept about ourselves. We may want to imagine that we are forgiving people but when we see what forgiveness really is, we balk.

Thus, the Christian Church created a theory of atonement whereby Jesus suffers the wrath of God in our place in order to satisfy a desire for justice within God, because we love justice more than mercy. Such a theory is rooted in our desire to justify the wrath we pour upon those who do harm to us. If God is just and makes others suffer for the way that they have made him suffer, then we can feel righteous about making others suffer for the harm they have done to us. We want a god who is forgiving toward us but not forgiving toward those who do harm to us, or those we deem unworthy of forgiveness. Hence, we create a schizophrenic god who both suffers the offense without retaliation in an act of forgiveness (Jesus), and a wrathful God (The Father) who demands that someone suffer the offense even if it be his own son. How can such a god be one? How can a god who pours forth wrath upon his own son because of his offended honor be a loving god? In order to fall in love with the kind of Divinity that Jesus reveals we must know that when Jesus suffers his Father suffers as well. To believe the contrary, that god is pouring forth his wrath upon Jesus instead of you, makes loving such a god impossible.

If someone promised you eternal love but would torture you eternally if you did not respond properly to that love, it is not love they are promising. We could respond to a god who makes such an offer in obedience but never in love. Of course, our relationship with God never begins with love. Our initial, inherited understanding is always one of obedience, and love for God is always out of a second truth that we are coming into through our own authentic experience in God's divine presence.

Certainly, there is talk of both forgiveness and justice in the Scripture and sadly we read and attribute both as part of the objective nature of God, but the other way to read it is that justice is the place we begin—it is our foundational understanding—but forgiveness is the place God is calling us to. It is part of the second truth that we are always moving toward but can never really take in fully—it is the great mystery of God's mercy. That, however, does not mean that God's mercy eliminates the possibility of eternal separation from God's presence. God's mercy allows for that since to force people who hate mercy to live eternally in its presence would be torturous, and a loving God cannot be a torturous God.

The God that Jesus reveals, however, is always loving and forgiving and the only thing we have to do is to be willing to receive that love and forgiveness. We are safe in God because of who God is and not because of what we do. That is the whole point of Jesus and the cross, but we always want to add something that we must do in order to make ourselves feel worthy and better than others, especially those whom we do not love. Because of our lack of love for the whole of creation, we create theologies that convince us that God loves only portions of his creation and thus we are justified in loving only portions of it as well. We never seem to get beyond our tribalism, and whoever does is branded a heretic in order to preserve the illusion that God is like us and loves some more than others. If we were ever able to allow the things that Jesus said and did to change our understanding, we would see that Jesus is the ultimate heretic.

POSTSCRIPT

Truth, Meaning, and Hermeneutics in the 21st Century

LIKE ALL CONCEPTS, our concept of truth has changed over the course of time. One of the reasons for this is that our understanding of the human condition changes over time. When we thought that our experience was simply data recorded upon a *tabula rasa* or interpreted through a God-given, universal understanding or mental hardware, it was easy to believe that a proposition like "the grass is green" was true if it corresponded to the observable reality that the grass was in fact green. This idea of truth as correspondence had been around for a long time, but in the modern period of the 17th and 18th centuries it took a particularly radical form. The notion was that truth should be objective or have nothing to do with our subjective opinions or theories about things. Thus, the modern period was marked by a general rejection of theory in both science and theology. Aristotle's conceptual understanding of the world had dominated the medieval period but many modern thinkers thought that simple observation had been neglected in favor of the authority of Aristotle's theories. Francis Bacon (1561-1626) suggested that we reject not only the theories of Aristotle but all theory in favor of simple observation.

Similarly, the early Christians thought that there was a need for a theory about how to read the scripture since what Jesus said seemed so radically different from the Jewish tradition; yet, Jesus confirms the God-inspired nature of the Jewish Scripture. What early Christians sought as a solution was to read the ancient text on an allegorical level and find a deeper meaning that was more compatible with what Jesus said and did. This required a theory of interpretation, and several emerged in the ancient and medieval world. Luther and the reformers, however, like Bacon, rejected the idea of theory. Luther claimed that Scripture read literally and infused by the Holy Spirit provided us access to its authorial intent.

Thus, both modern science and reformation theology pointed toward facticity as the basis for truth. For both science and theology, this seemed to be a way to avoid theory. Today, however, we know much more about our human condition. We now know that such an early modern view was itself a theory. Human experience is always theory-laden, and we process the data of our experience through the conceptual filters that theories provide, whether we are aware of it or not. Since we receive these concepts and theories uncritically at an early age it is easy to naively assume they reflect the way things actually are rather than merely the way past generations have chosen to understanding and interpret their experience. A 21st century education should remove this naiveté but many people continue to insist that our experience is like that of the rest of the animal kingdom and based upon some God-given or natural hardware through which we process the data of our experience. True, other crea-tures, without culture, history, or language, simply read their experience through whatever understanding nature has supplied. The rest of the animal kingdom may alter their understanding through their experience, but without human culture, history, and language, they do not pass on those altered understandings to future generations the way we do. Consequently, we are not only interpretative beings but what marks and distinguishes our interpretive nature is that we have inherited our interpretations from sources human rather than divine.

The Truth of Our Understanding

In the past when we imagined that we simply perceived the world as given data, or that we interpreted it through God-given hardware, it was easy to treat the world simply as data. Today, we know that the world, as we have been taught to interpret it, is largely a social construct that we have inherited from human sources. This gives us the freedom to rethink the understanding out of which we create our interpretations of our experience. In the past, we generally came to question our understanding only when anomalies appeared and our inherited understanding failed to provide an interpretation that made sense. Today, how-ever, for those who are aware of the hermeneutic nature of our human condition a general suspicion concerning our inherited understanding is always with us.

Consequently, for those with a 21st century understanding of our human condition it has become an extremely philosophical age. Our early modern ancestors may have focused on developing methods to test the truth of data, but today we are much more aware of how the data is affected by the understanding through which we interpret it. Questioning the understanding rather than the data is a philosophical rather than a scientific project. Of course, not everyone is aware of the hermeneutic nature of our human condition and consequently many do not question their inherited understanding. Many theists, in spite of all the evidence to the contrary, believe that God, rather than our human communities, has equipped us with the conceptual orientation through which we interpret our experience, and therefore there is no reason to seek a better conceptual perspective. This is what lies at the root of so much of the religious fundamentalism that we see throughout the world. Likewise, many atheists are content with their inherited understanding, since in the absence of God, human beings are the measure of all things, and if the scientific community settles on a particular conceptual understanding there is no reason to question it.

In spite of the dominance of these two groups of people, civilization continues to advance because of the avant-garde, the heretic, and the outsider whom society tries to marginalize. The advance of science is not simply a matter of discovering new data, but more the result of innovative ways of thinking about the data. Copernicus does not tell us about what is out-there, but how we should conceptualize what is out-there. Likewise, Newton, Darwin, Freud, and Einstein all tell us the same thing. We judge such theories true, not because they correspond to data, but because they give us a more fruitful interpretation of the data. Indeed, our theories are not part of the data, but belong to the understanding through which we process the data.

Our modern thinking may have equated truth with facticity, but that was because the relative nature of the understanding through which we interpret the facts was unknown to us. Now that we know that our interpretation of facts is relative to the historic, cultural, and linguistic understanding we bring to the data of our experience, we must question the truth of that understanding. When we equated truth with facticity we had easy access to it through observation and experiment, but when we speak of the ultimate truth of our understanding it always eludes our grasp because there is always an alternative and perhaps better way to perceive things. This is why the second truth is infinitely knowable, because there is the constant hope that there is a still better way to conceptualize what we wish to know. This is what lies behind nearly all intellectual and spiritual advances. It is the mystical truth that led Copernicus to rethink how we conceptualize the heavens, and what caused Kant to rethink how we conceptualize our human experience. And it is the truth that led Augustine, Francis, and Luther to rethink the Gospel.

Intellectual or Spiritual Journeys

What makes those who are on an intellectual or spiritual journey different from the practitioners of both science and religion is that the truth for them is not something to which they have easy access. It is always that mysterious thing that leads them on in the journey. Seekers of such truth are different than those who claim to possess the truth, because for them the truth is always something greater than their present understanding. Instead of enjoying the false security that comes from believing that they possess the truth, they seek a truth that tells them there is a still better way to understand their experience of the world, other people, themselves, and God. For such individuals, truth is what drives them to want to know that other person more intimately or that piece of art more deeply. It is not more information that they are after but a better perspective through which to interpret what the data, or that other person, or that piece of art is saying. In order to do so they must let the data of their experience change the understanding through which they are interpreting that data. When they allow the data to change their understanding, they come to a new perspective that can open them to data that had previously been hidden or concealed by their old understanding.

Most religious people, like most scientific people, equate the truth with their own understanding and think of the two as synonymous. They insist that the data must conform to their accepted understanding, and they judge whether something is true or false by its conformity to the way they had been taught to interpret the world. By contrast, Socrates' students and Jesus' disciples allowed their experiences with Socrates and Jesus to change their understanding in order to get a better interpretation of the things that Socrates or Jesus said and did. Once our understanding is changed by such experiences, we have a new understanding through which to read and interpret our future experiences. This is the nature of the hermeneutic circle (or hermeneutic spiral) by which the data of our experience changes the understanding through which we interpret our experience and therein are brought to a new interpretation. But even that new understanding must be open to being changed by the data in order to bring us into ever new interpretations. Human history has progressed because certain individuals abandoned the security offered by their inherited orientation and set out on intellectual or spiritual journeys to discover better ways to conceptualize what they were experiencing.

In addition to being a major impetus behind human history, this hermeneutic circle is also what lies at the base of any real attempt at human intimacy. When we encounter others whom we wish to know intimately, we have to let what they say and do change our conceptual understanding so that we come closer to their perspective. Real intimacy is largely a matter of coming to see how others conceptualize and thus interpret their experience. When I am with persons whom I wish to really know, and they say to me, "That's not what I mean," they are trying to get me to change my conceptual perspective to something closer to their own so I might understand why they interpret things as they do. Likewise, when an art professor explains a piece of art, or a philosophy professor explains a particular philosopher's position, they are trying to get us to see what the artist or philosopher sees. They are trying to get us to see something that is hidden from our old understanding.

People who cling to their inherited understanding are generally not open to anything but the most conventional art or philosophy. They imagine that their inherited perspective represents the only true conceptual understanding and what does not conform to it is simply not true. This narrow mindedness has a devastating effect upon our attempts at intimacy, since it demands that all who wish to commune with us do so from our limited perspective. Our narrow mindedness causes us to be in relationships only with those who share our perspective, and if it is revealed that someone has a different perspective than our own, our interest in them wanes. Real intimacy, however, involves the penetration into another's unique perspective. When a spouse is bothered by something that would not bother the other spouse, compassion requires that the unaffected spouse attempt to perceive the situation from a perspective that is not their own.

Likewise, when your child is scared by something that we as adults have no fear of, the compassionate parent tries to see the circumstance from the child's perspective and therein feel what the child feels. In the case of young children, they are often frightened because their foundational understanding and the security it provides is not yet in place. To feel what the child feels, we have to suspend the understanding through which we normally process the data of our experience and attempt to take on the way they perceive and interpret the world.

Of course, modernity told us that there was no such truth concerning an individual's perspective but all truth was common, objective, and factual. That contributed greatly to an inhuman age of fascism, totalitarianism, and fundamentalism where the truth of the individual was suppressed. Although suppressed, however, the second truth of the individual cannot be denied since it is at the base of the advance of human history and perhaps more importantly at the base of human intimacy as well.

The Great Insights of Our Day

Recent centuries have brought us to an awareness of the fact that our human condition is more mysterious than previously imagined. We now know that we are often motivated by what is below the level of our conscious mind and that our behavior is often connected to causes of which we are unaware. Likewise, we now know that causality itself is not as simple and linear as we would like to imagine, and butterflies flapping their wings can have a causal effect upon tsunamis. Perhaps the greatest insight of our day, however, is that our human experience is hermeneutic: that is, a reading or interpretation created out of the prejudices that constitute our conceptual understanding. In light of these insights, the psychologist tries to make us aware of things that affect our thinking and behavior, which are beneath the conscious level of our awareness; and the contemporary physicist explains the world with concepts very different from those used when we had a mechanical view of the universe and we imagined simple linear causal connections. Likewise, today's philosophers and spiritual directors should make us aware of the prejudicial concepts through which we filter and interpret the data of our experience in order that we might pursue greater perspectives than those we inherit.

Immanuel Kant (1724-1804) was the first to explain the filtered or phenomenal nature of our experience. Kant's insight came on the heels of David Hume's skepticism. In the middle of the great Enlightenment of the 18th century, David Hume (1711-1776) discovered that certain key ideas which he had taken for true could not be traced back to an actual experience. Hume consequently concluded that such ideas were the product of the imagination and not rooted in actual experience. Kant saw this as a great threat to human knowledge and sought to solve the problem by arguing that it was not the imagination that gave us such ideas but rather they were part of the innate hardware through which the mind processed the data of our experience. Although philosophers before him knew that there had to be something within the mind that processed the data of our experience, what Kant showed was that it was much more extensive than what anyone had previously imagined. Before Kant, we thought that our ideas of things like cause and effect, or time and space, came to us as part of the data of our experience, but Kant argued that such ideas were part of an innate mental hardware through which we processed the data.

That was a revolutionary step since it meant that we never experience the objective world or things as they are in themselves (what Kant called the noumenal world), but rather a world shaped by the innate mental hardware through which we interpret the data of our experience (what Kant called the phenomenal world). That meant that human knowledge was limited and we could not know things as they were in themselves but only as we experienced them. Kant, however, did think that he was saving human knowledge from Hume's skepticism, since this mental hardware was universal and the way all human beings process the data of their experience. The next two centuries, however, would reveal that we bring much more to the data of our experience than the native hardware that Kant had described, and human knowledge was hardly as universal as Kant had imagined.

With the 19th century, we became aware of historicism and the fact that the understanding by which we process the data of experience was also filtered by an understanding that was not native to the mind but changes with historical epochs and the vicissitudes of time. Albert Einstein did not have the same understanding that Isaac Newton had concerning the physical universe, nor do physicists today have the same interpretive understanding Einstein had. Equally, a psychologist in the 21st century does not have the same conceptual understanding through which to filter her experience that Freud had at the beginning of the 20th century. The understanding through which we interpret the world changes over time.

In addition to historicism, the advent of cultural anthropology along with a greater knowledge of linguistics brought about an awareness of the enormous effect that our culture and language community have upon the understanding through which we interpret our experience. Thus the world that we experience is more than simply phenomenal, as Kant had imagined. The twenty-first century world is hermeneutic in that it is an interpretation or reading of the data of our experience based upon the historical, cultural, and linguistic biases within the understanding through which we interpret that data. None of us possesses a God's-eye-view. We are interpretative beings, and our

interpretations are shaped by concepts created by past generations and passed onto us through our history, culture, and language community. It may have been natural in the past to trust
our interpretations and treat them as given reality, since we do
not experience a distinction between the data of our experience
and the understanding through which we interpret it. Today,
however, that is a difficult position to maintain, since we no
longer believe that our experience is simply given but is rather a
composite of both the data and the understanding that processes
and interprets the data.

In the past, because we were unaware of this complex
nature of human experience, we treated every new insightful
interpretation in science or theology as if we had finally arrived
at the truth rather than simply a new interpretation because
of the new understanding we were bringing to the data of our
experience. Today, it would seem naïve to believe that our
present understanding provides the ultimate perspective. There
are always new and better ways to conceptualize our experience and therein reveal things previously hidden. That, however, does not undermine the idea of truth or our pursuit of it.
It merely reveals that the notion of truth we inherited from our
early modern ancestors was a terribly truncated notion and there
is a truth that is more personal and mysterious than the narrow
concept we have inherited.

Such a 21st century understanding has enormous conse-
quences upon theology. Most of Jesus' teachings have nothing to
do with factual truths. No one believes that the parables actually
took place. They are not factual but perspectival. What Jesus

offers is not some objective truth, but the very personal perspective that was his understanding. The Apostle Paul seems to have understood this for he says, "Let the same mind be in you that was in Christ Jesus."[84] In that regard, Jesus is not presenting us with a religion but a perspective for anyone on a spiritual journey, regardless of their religion. There is, however, the other part of the Jesus revelation that has been made into a religion since Jesus not only tells us who we should be in relationship to the Divine, but he also tells us of the nature of the Divine. Of course, what he tells us about the nature of the Divine is very different from what most religions that bear his name tell us. Jesus tells us that God perceives the prodigal son with the same degree of love as the good son,[85] the one who worked only the last hour as the same as those who labored all day.[86] He tells us that there is more joy in heaven over one repentant sinner than over ninety-nine righteous,[87] and we should be like our heavenly Father who is "kind to the ungrateful and the wicked."[88] He is presenting us with a very radical picture of God that the world has yet to take in.

Likewise, Jesus gives us an equally radical picture of how we should perceive ourselves in relationship to Divine. He tells us we should perceive the God of the universe as either "our father," "your father," or "your heavenly father."[89] Jesus is not

---

84. Philippians 2:5.
85. Luke 15:11-32.
86. Matthew 20:1-16.
87. Luke 15:7.
88. Luke 6:35.
89. Matthew 5:16; 5:45; 5:48; 6:1; 6:4; 6:6; 6:8; 6:9; 6:15; 6:14;

speaking about objective truth here. God did not create us by impregnating a female the way humans become a father. Rather Jesus is telling us how we should understand and interpret our God experiences. When Jesus says, "I am the way and the truth,"[90] he is speaking of the perspectival truth through which he interpreted his experience and through which we should interpret our experience as well. Sadly, as many times as Jesus says, "Follow me" throughout the Gospels,[91] followers of Jesus generally do not take that to mean that they are to take on the Jesus perspective and turn the other check,[92] or love their enemies and pray for those who persecute them.[93] Instead, they make following Jesus into believing certain doctrinal truths, but professing a belief in certain object truths does not give us access to the Gospel. We only really begin to see the Gospel when we view it through the Jesus perspective.

The truth of the Gospel is encountered only through faith, and the kind of faith Jesus is talking about has nothing to do with theological doctrines. The kind of faith Jesus is speaking of is perhaps best understood as simply a matter of taking on the mind of Christ and seeing things as Jesus sees them. When Jesus

6:18; 6:26; 6:32; 7:11; 10:20; 10:29; 18:14; 18:35; Mark 11:25; Luke 6:36; 10:21; 11:13; 12:30; 12:32; 15:21; John 8:41; 20:17.

90.   John 14:6.

91.   Matthew 4:19; 8:22; 9:9; 16:24; 19:21; Mark 2:14; 8:34; 10:21; Luke 5:27; 9:23; 9:59; 18:22; John 1:43; 10:27; 12:26; 13:36; 21:19.

92.   Matthew 5:39.

93.   Matthew 5:44.

points out the great faith of the Canaanite woman[94] or the Roman centurion,[95] what he sees in them is that they have the same perspective that he has. Jesus sees that God takes care of even the dogs and the Canaanite woman has come to the same perspective. Likewise, Jesus sees himself as under God's authority, just as the Roman centurion has the same understanding regarding authority. Great faith is a matter of getting a glimpse of the Jesus perspective and making it our own.

As we take on more and more of the Jesus perspective we begin to see ourselves, the world, and God in a way that our old understanding would not allow us to see. Our inherited understanding only allows us to see so much. In order to see more, the understanding through which we interpret our experience has to change. As it does, new vistas open before us. This is the nature of the hermeneutic circle whereby we allow the data of the experience to do violence to our old understanding and therein open us to the possibility of a new perspective which can make better sense of the data. If we allow them, the things that Jesus says and does should do violence to our old understanding and therein allow us to go deeper and deeper into the mind of Christ.

Regrettably, many who consider themselves followers of Jesus never come to pursue the unique perspective which is Jesus' second truth. Instead, they imagine that all they need to know of Jesus is what they have learned through their inherited, foundational understanding. Since they have never ventured out in search of a second truth themselves, they cannot

94. Matthew 15:21-28.
95. Matthew 8:5-10.

imagine a second truth in Jesus. So, their foundational understanding becomes sacred and the means by which they judge
everything. Thus, when Jesus says and does things that do not
conform to their foundational orientation, they create theologies
that defend, not what Jesus is saying, but their own understanding. By contrast, those who have entered into a spiritual journey
of following Jesus allow their understanding to change in order
to come closer and closer to the Jesus perspective, which is the
new wine that bursts the old wineskin.[96]

Unfortunately, the Jesus perspective is not for everyone.
Most people do not want a truth that does violence to their
understanding. They want an understanding that can repel such
an assault and thereby provide the kind of security they get from
believing that they know how to interpret their experience cor-
rectly. But such a sense of security comes from a faith in our own
understanding, and real faith always comes from our connection
to something greater than ourselves and our understanding.

A 21st Century Understanding of Truth

We are hermeneutic creatures who are defined by the prejudices through which we interpret the data of our lives. These
prejudices also go a long way in determining the quality of our
lives, but we all too often naively imagine that they are not prejudices at all but part of a given reality. Of course, in a sense
they are given, but they do not come to us the way the data
of our experience come. The physical world provides pure data

---

96. Matthew 9:17, Mark 2:22, and Luke 5:37.

independent of human influence, but the human world provides us with the understanding through which to interpret that data. Since we have been taught to interpret our experience by other human beings whose judgments and conventions we inherit at an early age before we can critically question them, they easily become that sacred understanding through which we interpret everything.

There are the few, however, who do eventually come to authenticate themselves and stand out from the herd to the extent that they question and change their inherited conceptual understanding in the hope of coming to a more transparent and fruitful interpretation of their experience. This is not easily accomplished. To authenticate ourselves is a lonely process and most choose not to be separated from the way everyone else is thinking. Indeed, it is often dangerous to do so, since those with authentic understandings are often labeled heretics or crazies. In the past, when we thought that reality was simply given rather than perspectival and interpretive, it seemed right to see those who rejected the conventional understanding as simply wrong, heretical, or crazy. Today, however, we should be able to see that some of those people were neither wrong, nor crazy but rather authentic individuals who sensed a greater truth than the truth they inherited from sources all too human.

Our Enlightenment ancestors may have told us that we could simply lay down our prejudices and receive our experience as an objective given, but we now know that is unrealistic. Our experience will always be an interpretation created out of the prejudices of our conceptual understanding. That might at first seem to undermine any attempt we might make toward truth, but we should now understand that it only undermined a certain, unrealistic concept of truth. Furthermore, that unrealistic concept of objective truth has never been the concept of truth that has possessed and motivated the most interesting and courageous of human beings. That might have been the concept from which we attempt to draw some sense of security, but human history has advanced, both intellectually and spiritually, because certain individuals sought a better way to conceptualize their experience than through their inherited concepts. Such individuals, however, have usually paid a great price since they pose a serious threat to those who see their own understanding as sacred truth.

We have long been aware of a tension between people because of differences of race, religion, class, or gender but perhaps the greatest tension exists between people with these two very different ideas of truth. It may be rooted in different stages of life and even different hemispheres of the brain, but both truths serve essential functions and are deeply tied to the reality of our human condition. The first truth is the product of human judgment and convention but it is essential to our early development and wellbeing that we see it as absolute truth. We need to believe that we have a firm foundation upon which to begin to build a healthy sense of identity. The other truth usually does not appear until later in life and often only after something has happened to shake our initial, foundational truth. Unlike the foundational truth with which we begin, this second truth is not something we can know or possess. It is, as we have said, forever out of reach, but, as an end or *telos* that draws us on in our intellectual or spiritual journey, it is as much a part of our human condition as the foundational truth with which we begin.

Another name for this second truth is philosophy. Science and religion may tell us how things work and how we should interpret our experience. But, philosophy makes us suspicious of that understanding because it has been awakened to a more divine truth that is always out of reach but always worth pursuing. Some never become aware of this second, philosophical truth and they treat the understanding they received as their initial orientation as sacred and, therefore, in little need of correction. Others, however, enter into the intellectual and spiritual journey that is philosophy and begin to search for a better way to conceptualize and interpret their experience.

Bibliography

Benardete, Seth. *The Being of the Beautiful*. Chicago, IL: University of Chicago Press, 1984.

Descartes, René. *Discourse on the Method*. Translated by Elizabeth S. Haldane and G. R. T. Ross. Philosophical Works of Descartes vol.1. New York: Dover, 1955.

Gadamer, Han Georg. *Truth and Method*. Translated by Joel Weinsheimer and Donald G. Marshall. New York: Continuum, 1999.

Heidegger, Martin. *Being and Time*. Translated by John Macquarrie and Edward Robinson. New York: Harper and Row, 1962.

Huxley, Aldous. *The Doors of Perception*. New York: HarperCollins Publishers, 2004.

James. William. *The Will to Believe and Other Essays in Popular Philosophy*. New York: Dover, 1956.

Locke, John. *An Essay Concerning Human Understanding*. Edited by Peter H. Nidditch. Oxford: Clarendon, 1975.

Noddings, Nel. *Caring: A Feminine Approach to Ethics and Moral Education*. Berkeley CA: University of California Press, 2003.

Ortega y Gasset, Jose. *On Love: Aspects of a Single Theme*. Translated by Toby Talbot. New York: Penguin, 1957.

Plato. *Apology*. Translated by Hugh Tredennick. In *The Collected Dialogues of Plato*, edited by Edith Hamilton and Huntington Cairns. Princeton, NJ: Princeton University Press, 1989.

————. *Crito.* Translated by Hugh Tredennick. In *The Collected Dialogues of Plato*, edited by Edith Hamilton and Huntington Cairns. Princeton, NJ: Princeton University Press, 1989.

————. *Meno.* Translated by W. K. C. Guthrie. In *The Collected Dialogues of Plato*, edited by Edith Hamilton and Huntington Cairns. Princeton, NJ: Princeton University Press, 1989.

Ross, Maggie. *Writing the Icon of the Heart: In Silence Beholding.* Eugene, OR: Cascade Books (An Imprint of Wipf and Stock Publishers), 2013.

Whitehead, Alfred North. *The Concept of Nature.* New York: Cosimo Classics, 2007.

Wittgenstein, Ludwig. *Philosophical Investigations.* Translated by G. E. M. Anscombe. New York: Macmillan, 1968.